Preface

LCI. 12/.

This bibliography is essentially a list of manuals and other publications that outline, in more or less detail, the organization of national governments. An understanding of the functions and organization of a government may enable the researcher and the librarian to trace major government programs and publications about specific activities to the pertinent government departments and agencies.

Unfortunately, detailed and current manuals outlining functions of individual agencies and their subdivisions are rare. We have, therefore, also included in the present bibliography works of a more general scope that describe the history and often the legislative background of government agencies and bibliographies which may lead the researcher to other sources of information on governmental organization.

For some countries even the existence of an agency or a change in its name or organizational classification may be difficult to ascertain. Supplemental sources of information in such instances include official gazettes, national budgets, lists of corporate author headings, and, last but not least, city and telephone directories.

This bibliography is in many ways a followup and a supplement to *Government Publications: A Guide to Bibliographic Tools* (Washington, Library of Congress, 1975) which provides information on bibliographic control of government publications for 140 countries and 60 international intergovernmental organizations and includes entries for over 3,000 bibliographic works.

The first part of this bibliography includes basic works on public administration and governmental organization in general, manuals, handbooks, and yearbooks containing concise information on the organization of national governments worldwide or for certain geographic areas and a number of helpful bibliographies.

The second part lists individual countries in alphabetical order, citing organizational manuals, wherever available, and other publications containing general information on the governmental organization of each country. Selected retrospective sources, which provide information on past changes within individual governments, are also included.

The materials included in this bibliography have been selected mainly from the collections of the Library of Congress. Entries and call numbers are those used in the Library of Congress card catalog. In a few instances,

iii

however, works that could not be located in the Library of Congress were included. The index to the bibliography includes personal and corporate authors, selected titles of works, and names of geographical areas and countries.

Inevitably, important sources of information on the organization of national governments have been overlooked, and errors—especially in the determination of dates for the beginning and end of periods of publication of serials—have been made. Question marks are used to indicate that precise dates could not be ascertained. Corrections of errors, as well as suggestions of additional sources of information, will therefore be greatly appreciated.

VLADIMIR M. PALIC

GOVERNMENT ORGANIZATION MANUALS

A Bibliography

Compiled by V<small>LADIMIR</small> M. P<small>ALIC</small>

Serial Division, Reference Department

LIBRARY OF CONGRESS   WASHINGTON   1975

gov Doc

Library of Congress Cataloging in Publication Data

Palic, Vladimir M
  Government organization manuals.

   1. Public administration—Bibliography.   I.   Title.
Z7164.A2P33   [JF1341]   016.351   75–26755
ISBN 0–8444–0171–4

For sale by the Superintendent of Documents, U.S. Government Printing Office
Washington, D.C. 20402. Price $1.40

Stock No. 030–001–00071–1/Catalog No. LC1.12/2:G74

Contents

Public administration in general

Research in governmental organization necessarily requires knowledge of the theory of public administration and of basic principles of governmental organization. The various forms of modern governmental systems and the lack of uniformity in administrative terminology further complicate the understanding of the organization of governments.

The following are a few works that may help the interested researcher:

1
Alderfer, Harold F.   Public administration in newer nations. New York, Praeger [1967] 206 p. (Praeger special studies in international politics and public affairs)   JF51.A56

2
Bibliographie de science administrative, 1967–1970. Paris, Centre de documentation, Sciences humaines [1972?] 222 p. (Collection Documentation)   Z7164.A2B5
    Beginning in 1971, kept up to date in *Bulletin signalétique 528: Science administrative.*

3
Dimock, Marshall E., *and* Gladys O. Dimock.   Public administration. 4th ed. New York, Holt, Rinehart and Winston [1969] 634 p.   JF1351.D5 1969
    Deals extensively with U.S. governmental organization.

4
Gladden, Edgar N.   An introduction to public administration. 4th ed. London, Staple Press, 1966. xxxv, 260 p.   JF1351.G53 1966
    Deals extensively with British governmental organization.

5
Hodgson, John S.   Public administration. New York, McGraw-Hill [1969] 312 p.
                                                                         JF1351.H6
    Deals mainly with Canadian governmental organization.

6
United Nations. *Public Administration Division.*   United Nations directory of national agencies and institutions for the improvement of public administration. New York, 1970. 129 p. ([United Nations. Document] ST/TAO/M/47)
                                                    JX1977.A2 ST TAO/M/47
For information on current developments in the field of public administration science, the following publications will be helpful:

7
Annuaire international de la fonction publique. 1970/71+ Paris, Institut international d'administration publique.   JA1.A1A55
    Issued as a supplement to: Institut international d'administration publique. *Bulletin.*

8
Institut international d'administration publique. Bulletin. Jan./Mar. 1967+ Paris.
    quarterly.   JA1A1I58

9
International review of administrative sciences. v. 1+ 1928+ Brussels, International
    Institute of Administrative Sciences.   JA1.A1I6

10
Public administration. v. 1+ Jan. 1923+ London. Institute of Public Administration.
    quarterly.   JA8.P8

11
Public administration review. v. 1+ autumn 1940+ [Chicago] bimonthly.   JK1.P85
    Published by the American Society of Public Administration.

GENERAL MANUALS

12
International yearbook and statesmen's who's who. 1953+ London, Burke's Peerage.
                                                                                  JA51.I57

13
Political handbook and atlas of the world. Jan. 1, 1927+ New York, Harper & Row,
    for Council of Foreign Relations. annual.   JF37.P6
        Since 1971, a supplement to the 1970 edition is issued annually under the
    title *The World This Year* (New York, Simon and Schuster. JF37.W65).

14
The Statesman's year-book; statistical and historical annual of the states of the world.
    1st+ 1864+ London, New York, St. Martin's Press.   JA51.S7

15
U.S. *Central Intelligence Agency.* Chiefs of state and cabinet members of foreign
    governments. [Washington] monthly.   JF37.U5

REGIONAL MANUALS

16
Africa South of the Sahara. 1971+ London, Europa Publications. annual.
                                                                                  DT351.A37

17
Annuaire de l'Afrique du Nord. 1+ 1962+ [Paris] Centre national de la recherche
    scientifique.   DT181.A74

18
Annuaire des états d'Afrique noire, gouvernements et cabinets ministériels, partis
    politiques [1961]+ Paris, Édiafric.   JQ3194.A63

19
L'Annuaire du grand Maghreb arabe. The Great Arabic Maghreb annual. 1+ 1965/66+ Tunis, Imp. al-Asrin. DT181.A745
In Arabic, English and French.

20
Bidwell, Robin L. The Arab world, 1900–1972. London, F. Cass [1973] 124 p. (*His* Guide to government ministers, v. 2) JQ1850.A4B53 1973

21
—— The British Empire and successor states, 1900–1972. London, F. Cass [1974] 156 p. (*His* Guide to government ministers, v. 3) JN248.B52 1974

22
—— The major powers and western Europe, 1900–1971. [London] F. Cass, [1973] 297 p. (*His* Guide to government ministers, v. 1) JN12.B5 1973

23
Carnegie Endowment for International Peace. *Library.* European governments in exile. Comp. by Helen L. Scanlon. [Washington, 1943] 24 p. (*Its* Memoranda series, no. 3. Revised January 25, 1943) JX1906.A35 no. 3a
"This memorandum attempts to set forth the organization, personnel, diplomatic activities and publications of the European governments which are now functioning outside their own territories."

24
États africains d'expression française et République malgache. 1962+ Paris, R. Julliard. JQ3191.A17

25
The Europa year book. 1st+ ed.; 1959+ London, Europa Publications. JN1.E85
"Replaces the loose-leaf *Europa Encyclopedia.*"

26
French West Africa. Annuaire du gouvernement général de l'Afrique occidentale française. [1903–22] Paris. JQ3357.A3

27
Gt. Brit. *Colonial Office.* Colonial reports-annual. no. 1–1936. London, H. M. Stationery Off., 1891–1940. 1936 v. JV33.G7A4
Superseded by its "Colonial annual reports" from 1946.

28
Gsovski, Vladimir, *and* Kazimierz Grzybowski. Government, law and courts in the Soviet Union and Eastern Europe. New York, Praeger, [c1959] 2 v. (xxxii, 2067 p.) DLC LL

29
Henderson, John W., *and others.* Area handbook for Oceania. [Washington, U.S. Govt. Print. Off.] 1971. xiv, 555 p. DU17.H45
"DA pam. no. 550–94."

30
The Middle East and North Africa. [1st]+ ed.; 1948+ London, Europa Publications. DS49.M5

31
Organization of American States. *General Secretariat.* Chiefs of state and cabinet ministers of the American Republics. Washington, D.C. quarterly   F1402.A228

32
The Pacific islands year book. [1st]+ ed.; 1932+ Sydney, Pacific Publications.
DU1.P15

33
La Politique africaine en 1969: Cameroun, RCA, Congo, Côte d'Ivoire, Dahomey, Gabon, Haute-Volta, Mali, Mauritanie, Niger, Sénégal, Tchad, Togo. 2. éd. Paris, Édiafric [1969?] 333 p.   JQ3353 1969.P6
"Numéro spécial du *Bulletin de l'Afrique noire.*"

34
Répertoire de l'administration africaine; Cameroun, RCA, Congo, Côte d'Ivoire, Dahomey, Gabon, Haute-Volta, Mali, Mauritanie, Niger, Sénégal, Tchad, Togo. 1. éd. Paris, Édiafric-La Documentation africaine [1971] 411 p.
"Numéro spécial du *Bulletin de l'Afrique noire.*"   JQ1874.R46

35
Stanford Research Institute. Area handbook for the Peripheral States of the Arabian Peninsula. Prepared for the American University. [Washington, U.S. Govt. Print. Off.] 1971. xiv, 201 p.   DS247.A14S78
"DA pam. 550–92."

36
Stoddard, Theodore L., *and others.* Area handbook for the Indian Ocean territories. Prepared for the American University by the Institute for Cross-Cultural Research. [Washington, U.S. Govt. Print. Off.] 1971. xvi, 160 p.
DT468.S76

37
U.S. *Library of Congress.* A guide to the official publications of the other American republics. Washington [1945–49] 19 v. (*Its* Latin American series, no. 9–11, 15, 17, 19, 22–25, 27, 29–31, 33–37)   Z1605.U64
Each volume is devoted to a particular country and includes a concise history of government agencies.

38
The West Indies and Caribbean year book. Anuario comercial de las Antillas y paises del Caribe. [1st]+ year; 1926/27+ London, T. Skinner.   F2131.W47
Includes a section on government for each country. Title varies.

39
Who's who in U.A.R. and the Near East. Cairo [1935–59?]   DT44.W47
Also includes Cyprus, Iraq, Jordan, Lebanon, Libya, Saudi Arabia, Sudan, Syria, and, from 1954, Aden, Ceylon, Ethiopia, India, Indonesia, and Pakistan.

40
A Year book of the Commonwealth. 1967+ London, H. M. Stationery Off.
JN248.C5912
Formerly called *Commonwealth Relations Office List* (1951–65), *Commonwealth Relations Office Yearbook* (1966), *Commonwealth Office Yearbook* (1967–68). It superseded the *India Office and Burma Office List* (1803–1947, JQ202.A3) and the *Colonial Office List* (1862–1966, called *Dominions Office and Colonial Office List* from 1926 to 1940, JV1005 and JV33.G7A3).

The following bibliographies will also be of assistance:

41
Alderfer, Harold F. A bibliography of African government, 1950–1966. [2d rev. ed.] Lincoln University, Pa., Lincoln University Press, 1967. 163 p.
Z3501.A6 1967

42
Centre d'analyse et de recherche documentaires pour l'Afrique noire. Afrique noire d'expression française: sciences sociales et humaines; guide de lecture. [Paris, 1969?] 301 p.
Z3501.C45

43
Mesa, Rosa Q. Bibliography of organization manuals and other sources of information on the governmental organization of the countries of Latin America. *In* Seminar on the Acquisition of Latin American Library Materials, *15th. University of Toronto, 1970*. Final report and working papers, v. 2. Working paper no. 16.
Z688.L4S38 15th, 1970

Individual countries

In addition to the general and regional manuals listed in the first part of this bibliography, there are handbooks and other publications, often issued in series, which may supplement information on governmental organization in individual countries. As examples, we may mention the following series published in the United States, in the USSR, and in France. The U.S. Department of the Army occasionally issues, in its pamphlet series no. 550, the so-called area handbooks prepared by the Foreign Area Studies Division of the American University in Washington. In the USSR, the Gosudarstvennoe izdatel'stvo fūridicheskoĭ literatury (State Publishing House of Legal Literature) issues manuals called *Gosudarstvennyĭ stroĭ* ... *(Government Organization of ...)* in its series Gosudarstvennyĭ stroĭ stran mira (Government organization in the countries of the world). In France, the series called "Comment ils sont gouvernés" (How they are governed), issued by Librairie générale de droit et de jurisprudence, presents data on governmental organization in individual countries. Some of these publications will be cited under respective countries where primary sources are not available or to supplement primary sources. For certain British Commonwealth countries or former British colonial possessions, the "Colonial annual reports," issued from 1946, and the numbered "Colonial reports-annual," issued before 1940, will be of assistance for retrospective administrative organization.

Generally, current or recent manuals will be listed first, followed by retrospective manuals and other sources of information.

AFGHANISTAN

44
The Kabul times annual. 1st+ ed.; 1967+ Kabul.   DS350.K32

45
Afghan general and commercial directory. 1948/49. [Karachi, S. M. Shah, Ministry of Commerce] 170 p.   DS351.A6
   Official section: p. 25–57.

46
Aleksandrov, Igor' A., *and* Roman T. Akhramovich. Gosudarstvennyĭ stroĭ Afganistana. Moskva, Gos. izd-vo fūrid. lit-ry, 1956. 59 p. (Gosudarstvennyĭ stroĭ stran mira)   JQ1763 1956.A75

7

47
Bhaneja, Balwant. Afghanistan: political modernization of a mountain kingdom.
    [New Delhi, Spectra Publications, 1973] 87 p.   JQ1765.A1B45
        Appendixes: A. Structure of Afghan government. –B. Composition of
    Afghan cabinets, 1963–72.

48
Gosudarstvennye i obshchestvenno-politicheskie deiàteli Afganistana. (Spravochnik).
    Moskva, "Nauka," 1967. 55 p.   JQ1764.G6
        A directory of government and political personalities.

49
Nursai, Ata M.   Materialien und Wege für eine Reform der staatlichen Verwaltungs-
    struktur in Afghanistan. [Köln] 1963. 91 p.   JQ1765.A1N8
        Materials relating to government reorganization. Includes a chart of the
    central government.

50
Smith, Harvey H., and others. Area handbook for Afghanistan. [Washington,
    U.S. Govt. Print. Off.] 1973. lvi, 453 p.   DS352.S55
    "DA pam. no. 550–65."

ALBANIA

51
Directory of Albanian officials. [n. p.] 1970. 121 p.   JN9684.D55

52
Keefe, Eugene K., and others.   Area handbook for Albania. [Washington, U.S.
    Govt. Print. Off.] 1971. xiv, 223 p.   DR701.S5K36
    "DA pam. no. 550–98."

53
Kuprits, Nikolaĭ IA.   Gosudarstvennyĭ stroĭ Narodnoĭ Respubliki Albanii. [Moskva]
    Izd-vo Moskovskogo Universiteta, 1960. 61 p.   JN9683 1960.K8

54
Skendi, Stavro, and others, ed.   Albania. London, Published for the Mid-European
    Studies Center of the Free Europe Committee, by Atlantic Press [1957]
    xiv, 389 p. (East Central Europe under the Communists)   DR701.S86S56 1957

ALGERIA

55
Merlo, Manuel.   L'organisation administrative de l'Algérie. 3. éd. rev. et mise à jour
    au 1er juin 1960. Blida, Impr. A. Mauguin, 1960. 217 p.   JQ3231.M4 1960

56
Nyrop, Richard F., and others.   Area handbook for Algeria. [2d revision. Washing-
    ton, U.S. Govt. Print. Off.] 1972. xiv, 401 p.   DT275.N9 1972
    "DA pam. no. 550–44."

57
Remili, Abderrahmane.   Les institutions administratives algériennes. Alger, Société
    nationale d'édition et de diffusion, [1967] 296 p.   JQ3231.R4

58
Sbih, Missoum. L'administration publique algérienne. [Paris, Hachette littérature, 1973] 378 p.　　　　DLC LL

ARGENTINA

59
García Zamor, Jean C. Public administration and social changes in Argentina 1943–1955. Rio de Janeiro [1968] xv, 190 p.　　　　JL2026 1943.G37

60
Munson, Frederick P., *and others*. Area handbook for Argentina. Washington, U.S. Govt. Print. Off., 1969. xiv, 446 p.　　　　F2808.M98
"DA pam. no. 550–73."

61
Organización Marka's. Guía interaction; administración pública. [Buenos Aires, Asesoramiento Empresario Integral, 1968] 1 v. (various pagings) JL2021.A3 1968

62
———— GUIAPA: Guía única integral administración pública argentina. [Buenos Aires, Organización Marcas, 1971]+ (looseleaf)　　　　JL2021.A3 1971
Contents: A. Orden nacional.

63
Orlandi, Héctor R. El poder ejecutivo argentino y el federalismo. Buenos Aires, Editorial Bibliográfica Argentina [1960] 110 p. (Libros científicos) JL2040.O74

AUSTRALIA

64
Australian government directory. 1973+ Canberra, Australian Govt. Pub. Service.
　　　　JQ4021.A23
Continues *Commonwealth of Australia Directory to the Office of the Governor-General, the Parliament, the Executive Government, the Judiciary, Departments and Authorities* (see below).

———

65
Australia. *Prime Minister's Dept.* Commonwealth of Australia directory to the Office of the Governor-General, the Parliament, the executive government, the judiciary, departments and authorities. 1926–[72] Canberra.　　　　JQ4021.A23
Title varies: 1926–58, *The Federal Guide.*

66
Crisp, Leslie F. Australian national government. [Croydon, Australia] Longman [1970] 519 p.　　　　JQ4018.C78 1970

67
Hughes, Colin A., *and* B. D. Graham. A handbook of Australian government and politics, 1890–1964. Canberra, Australian National University Press, 1968. xv, 635 p.　　　　JQ4031.H83

68
International Public Relations Pty. The governments of Australia: a political and departmental guide. Braddon, A.C.T., International Public Relations [1972?] 194 p.   JQ4021.I58 1972

69
Parliamentary handbook of the Commonwealth of Australia. Canberra, Commonwealth Parliamentary Library.   JQ4054.C3
    Issued since 1901. In each issue: "Ministries since the establishment of the Commonwealth."

70
Sawer, Geoffrey. Australian government today. [Rev. i. e. 9th ed. Melbourne] Melbourne University Press; London, New York, Cambridge University Press [1967] 125 p.   JQ4015 1967.S3

AUSTRIA

71
Österreichischer Amtskalender. 1+ Jahrg.; 1922+ Wien, Österreichische Staatsdruckerei.   JN1604.A32
    Superseded *Hof- und Staats-Handbuch* (see below).

72
Austria. Hof- und Staats-Handbuch des österreichischen Kaiserthumes. [1807–68] Wien, K. k. Hof- und Staats-Aerarial-Druckerey.   JN1604.A3
    Continued, until 1918, by *Hof- und Staats-Handbuch der österreichisch-ungarischen Monarchie* (v. 1–44, 1874–1918; J1604).

73
Handbuch des öffentlichen Lebens in Österreich. [1+] Aufl.; 1958+ Wien, A. Heinreich.   JN2017.H3

74
Oberleitner, Wolfgang. Politisches Handbuch Österreichs, 1945–1972. Wien, Österr. Bundesverl. [1972] 247 p.   JN2017.O2 1972

BAHAMAS

75
Bahamas handbook and businessman's annual. 1st+ ed.; 1960+ Nassau, E. Dupuch, Jr., Publications.   F1650.B3

76
Bahamas. Bahamas civil service list. Nassau. annual.   JL614.A25

77
Gt. Brit. *Colonial Office.* Bahamas; a report. 1946–[65?] London, H. M. Stationery Off.   F1651.G65

BAHREIN [BAHRAIN]

78
Bahrein. Administrative report for the years 1926–1937. [n. p.] 1937.   J693.B3R17

79
—— Report. Bombay, Times of India Press. [1945/46?]+ annual.   J605.B3R15

80
Stanford Research Institute. Area handbook for the Peripheral States of the Arabian
   Peninsula. Prepared for the American University. [Washington, U.S. Govt.
   Print. Off.] 1971. xiv, 201 p.   DS247.A14S78
      "DA pam. no. 550–92."
      The Gulf States: p. 125–152.

BANGLADESH   [before 1971: EAST PAKISTAN]

81
Bangla Desh documents. [New Delhi, Ministry of External Affairs, 1971] xxiv,
   719 p.   DS485.B492B347
      For pre-1971 listing, see Pakistan.

BARBADOS

82
Barbados. Civil list. Bridgetown. annual?   JL624.A3

83
Gt. Brit. *Colonial Office.* Annual report on Barbados. [1947–62/63?] London,
   H. M. Stationery Off. (*Its* Colonial annual reports)   F2041.A33

BELGIUM

84
Annuaire administratif et judiciaire de Belgique. Administratief en gerechtelijk
   jaarboek voor België. 94.+ année; 1967/68+ Bruxelles, Bruylant.   JN6105.A6
      Continues *Annuaire administratif et judiciaire de Belgique et de la capitale
      du royaume,* published from 1864.
      In Flemish and French.

85
Guide des ministères. Revue de l'administration belge. 1951+ Bruxelles. annual.
                                                                    JN6103.G8
—— [Supplément] 1.+ année; juil. 1951+ Bruxelles. monthly.
                                                               JN6103.G8 Suppl.

86
Qui cherchez vous? Registre d'adresses des départements d'administration générale
   ainsi que des services et institutions qui en dépendent. Namur, Éditions administratives U.G.A. [1965?]+ 1 v. (looseleaf)   JN6103.Q5
      Register of addresses of government agencies.

For retrospective listing and the government in exile (1940–44), see:

87
Belgium. *Ministère de l'intérieur.* Almanach royal officiel. [1840–1939?] Bruxelles.
                                                                       JN6105
      Not published for 1915–19.

88
Carnegie Endowment for International Peace. *Library.* European governments in
exile. Compiled by Helen L. Scanlon. [Washington, 1943] 24 p. (*Its* memoranda
series, no. 3. Revised January 25, 1943)   JX1906.A35 no. 3a
     Originally published in 1942.
     Belgium: p. 2–3.

BHUTAN

89
Coelho, V. H. Sikkim and Bhutan. New Delhi, Indian Council for Cultural Relations. [1970] 138 p.   DS485.S5C6
     Government and general administration: p. 86–97.

90
Harris, George L., *and others.* Area handbook for Nepal, Bhutan and Sikkim. 2d
ed. [Washington, U.S. Govt. Print. Off.] 1973. lxxx, 431 p.
                                           DS493.4.H37 1973
     "DA pam. no. 550–35."

91
Hecker, Hellmuth. Sikkim and Bhutan; die verfassungsgeschichtliche und politische
Entwicklung der indischen Himalaya-Protektorate. Hamburg, [Forschungsstelle
für Völkerrecht] Frankfurt/M, In Kommission beim A. Metzner Verlag, 1970.
73 p. (Darstellungen zur auswärtigen Politik, Bd. 9)   DS485.S5H4
     Constitutional and political developments in the Indian Himalayan pro-
     tectorates.

BOLIVIA

92
Bolivia. *Dirección de Organización Nacional.* Manual de organización y funciones
del Gobierno de Bolivia. La Paz, Secretaría Técnica de Administración, 1969.
207 p. (Instituto Superior de Administración Pública. Serie Estudios, no. 11)

93
Bolivia. *Dirección Nacional del Servicio Civil.* Guía de funciones del Gobierno
Central. La Paz, 1969. 2 v. (Instituto Superior de Administratión Pública. Serie
Estudios, no. 10)

94
American University, *Washington, D.C. Foreign Areas Studies Division.* Area handbook for Bolivia. Washington, 1963 [i.e. 1964] 714 p.   F3308.A7

95
Bolivia. *Consulado, London.* Official handbook to Bolivia. London, Selwyn & Blout
[1924] 112 p.   F3308.B62

96
Cleven, Nels A. N. The political organization of Bolivia. Washington, D.C., Carnegie
Institution of Washington, 1940. 253 p. (Carnegie Institution of Washington.
Publication no. 510)   F3321.C58
                                         AS32.A5 no. 510

BOTSWANA [before 1966: BECHUANALAND]

97
Central government directory. [Gaborone] Information Services of the Office of the
President [1971?]+ JQ2760.A4A3

98
Červenka, Zdenek. Republic of Botswana. A brief outline of its geographical set-
ting, history, economy and policies. Uppsala, Scandinavian Institute of African
Studies, 1970. 1 v. DT791.C47
Government: p. 26–28.

99
Gt. Brit. *Office of Commonwealth Relations.* Annual report on the Bechuanaland
Protectorate. 1946–[65?] London, H. M. Stationery Off. ([Gt. Brit. Colonial
Office] Colonial annual reports) DT791.A55

BRAZIL

100
Perfil. abril 1972+ [São Paulo, Sociedade Editorial Visão] JL2499.S199P4a
A survey of legislative, executive and judicial branches of the federal gov-
ernment included in v. 39, no. 2, July 19, 1971, of *Visão* (São Paulo.
AP66.V58) under the title "Perfil da administração federal." Published from
April 1972, as a separate publication (v. 1, no. 1, April 1972, no. 2, Aug.
1972).

101
Avellar, Hélio de Alcântara. História administrativa e econômica do Brasil. 1. ed.
[Rio de Janeiro] Fundação Nacional de Material Escolar, 1970 [i.e. 1971]
363 p. JL2424.A9

102
Brazil. *Departamento Administrativo do Serviço Publico.* Indicador da organização
administrativa do executivo federal. [1940–57?] Rio de Janeiro, Impr. nacional.
JL2442.A3

103
Brazil. *Departamento Administrativo do Serviço Publico. Serviço de Documentação.*
História administrativa do Brasil. [Rio de Janeiro?] 1962–? [6? v.]
JL2424.A5
Second edition began publication in 1965 (JL2424.A52).

104
————— —————— Orgãos da administração federal; endereços, telefones. [Rio de Janeiro,
1967] 216 p. JL2421.A3 1967

105
Brazil. *Laws, statutes, etc.* Administração federal; organização e reforma. Legislação
basica, legislação complementar, jurisprudência administrativa, atualização ate
31.12.1972. [Compilação de] Guido Ivan de Carvalho. São Paulo, Editora Revista dos Tribunais, 1973. 435 p. (Coleção RT legislação) DLC LL

106
Weil, Thomas E., *and others*. Area handbook for Brazil. [Washington, U.S.
    Govt. Print. Off.] 1971. xviii, 645 p.   F2508.W44
    "DA pam. no. 550–20."

BULGARIA

107
U.S. *Central Intelligence Agency*. Directory of Bulgarian officials. [Washington]
    1972. 478 p.   JN9604.U54 1972
    Previous editions issued without author or publisher statement (JN9604.-
    D53).

108
U.S. *Embassy. Bulgaria*. Directory of Bulgarian government and party officials.
    [1969?]+ Sofia.   DLC

109
Aĭzenshtat, ÎA. I. Gosudarstvennyĭ stroĭ Narodnoĭ Respubliki Bolgarii. Moskva,
    Gos. izd-vo ŭrid. lit-ry, 1951. 287 p.   DLC LL

BURMA

110
American University, *Washington, D.C. Foreign Area Studies*. Area handbook
    for Burma. Co-authors: John W. Henderson [and others. Washington, U.S.
    Govt. Print. Off.] 1971. xiv, 341 p.   DS485.B81A348 1971
    "DA pam. no. 550–61."
    Chart of the Revolutionary Government: p. 152.

111
Burma. The quarterly civil list for Burma. [1900–48?]   JQ447 date b
    The annual volume of the civil list is called *History of Services of Gazetted
    and Other Officers*.

112
The India Office and Burma Office list. [1803–1947?] London, Harrison.
         JQ202.A3
    Continued by *The Commonwealth Relations Office List* (JN107.C6).

113
U.S. *Office of Strategic Services. Research and Analysis Branch*. The structure
    of the Government of Burma. [Washington] 1944. 53 p. (*Its* R & A no. 1713)
         UB250.U33 Rare Book Coll.

BURUNDI

114
Lemarchand, René. Rwanda and Burundi. London, Pall Mall Press, 1970. xiv,
    562 p. (Pall Mall library of African affairs)   DT449.R942L44 1970b

115
McDonald, Gordon C., *and others.* Area handbook for Burundi. Washington, U.S.
Govt. Print Off., 1969. xiv, 203 p. DT449.B8M3
"DA pam. no. 550–83."

116
Mpozagara, Gabriel. La République du Burundi. Paris, Berger-Levrault, 1971.
72 p. (Encyclopédie politique et constitutionnelle. Série Afrique) JQ3566.A5M5

CAMBODIA   see KHMER REPUBLIC

CAMEROON

117
Cameroon. *Ministry of Information and Tourism.* Annuaire national. National
year book. 1963+ [Douala, Édition Les 4 points cardinaux] JQ3521.A11A3

118
Gonidec, P. F. La République fédérale du Cameroun. Paris, Berger-Levrault,
1969. 88 p. (Encyclopédie politique et constitutionnelle. Série Afrique)
JQ3522.G6

119
Guid' Cameroun. 1959–[64?] Paris, Diloutremer. DT563.G8

120
Nelson, Harold D., *and others.* Area handbook for the United Republic of
Cameroon. [Washington, U.S. Govt. Print. Off.] 1974. xiv, 335 p. DT564.N44
"DA pam. no. 550–166."

121
Rubin, Neville N. Cameroun; an African federation. New York, Praeger [1971 i.e.
1972] 259 p. (Praeger library of African affairs) DT572.R84

CANADA

122
Canadian government programs and services reports. [Dec. 1973+] Don Mills,
Ontario, CCH Canadian Limited. looseleaf. JL5.C65 1973

123
Organization of the government of Canada. June 1958–[69?] Ottawa, Queen's
Printer, Dept. of Public Printing and Stationery JL5.O7
Since 1965 published in looseleaf form. French edition called: *L'Adminis-
tration fédérale du Canada* (JL5.A413). Not published from 1969 to 1974.
Resumed publication as 9th edition in 1974, with looseleaf amendments,
by Information Canada.

Other current and retrospective manuals:

124
Canada. *Bureau of Statistics.* The Canada year book. 1905+ Ottawa. HA744.S81

124a
Canada. *Privy Council.* Guide to Canadian ministries since confederation, July 1, 1867—April 1, 1973. Ottawa, Public Archives of Canada, 1974. 268 p.
JL97.C35 1974

124b
Canadian almanac & directory. [1st]+ year; 1848+ Toronto, Copp, Clark.
AY414.C2

125
The Canadian parliamentary guide. [1916?]+ Ottawa.   JL5.A4
    From 1867 to 1897(?), *Canadian Parliamentary Companion* (JL5.A3) included some information on government organization.

126
Corpus directory and almanac of Canada. 7th+ 1972+ Toronto, Corpus Publishers Services Ltd. annual.   F1004.7.M3
    Continuation of *McGraw-Hill Directory and Almanac of Canada,* published 1966–71.

127
Imperial year book for Dominion of Canada. 1914/15–? Montreal, Imperial Year-book.   F1008.I34

CENTRAL AFRICAN REPUBLIC [before 1960: UBANGI SHARI]

128
Kalck, Pierre. La République centrafricaine. Paris, Berger-Levrault, 1971. 52 p. (Encyclopédie politique et constitutionnelle. Série Afrique)   JQ3404.A3 1971

CEYLON   see SRI LANKA

CHAD

129
Annuaire officiel du Tchad. 1970+ Paris, Diloutremer.   JQ3405.A11A25
    Issued by the Direction générale de l'information, Chad.

130
Gonidec, P. F. La République du Tchad. Paris, Berger-Levrault, 1971. 79 p. (Encyclopédie politique et constitutionnelle. Série Afrique)   JQ3405.A3 1971.G6

131
Nelson, Harold D., *and others.* Area handbook for Chad. [Washington, U.S. Govt. Print. Off.] 1972. xiv, 261 p.   DT546.4.N44
    "DA pam. no. 550–159."

CHILE

132
Chile. *Departamento de Estudios Financieros.* Manual de la organización del Gobierno de Chile. [1957–59] Santiago de Chile, Tall. Gráf. "La Nación."
JL2602.A23

133
_____ Manual de la administración pública de Chile. 1959. [Santiago de Chile]
2 v.   JL2631.A3

134
_____ Organización institucional de Chile, 1955; legislación, funciones y organización de las instituciones fiscales, semifiscales, y autónomas del Estado. Santiago
de Chile, 1955. 2 v. (634 p.)   JL2615 1955.A52

135
Chile. *Ministerio de Hacienda.* Manual de la organización del Gobierno de Chile.
[1960. Santiago de Chile]   JL2631.A34
    Continuation of a publication with the same title issued by its Departa-
mento de Estudios Financieros for 1957–59 (see above).

136
Chile. *Ministerio del Interior.* Guía administrativa. [1893–1924?] Santiago de
Chile.   JL2602.A3

137
Guía de la administración pública de Chile y de los principales organismos del sector
privado. [1966–69?] Santiago [Ediciones Guía]   JL2621.G8

138
Prontuario administrativo de Chile según la nueva estructura de los servicios fiscales
e semifiscales de la República. [1943–57?] Santiago, Empresa Editora Atlas.
                                                                     JL2621.P7

139
Urzúa Valenzuela, Germán. Evolución de la administración pública chilena (1818–
1968). [Santiago de Chile] Editorial Jurídica de Chile [c1970] 277 p. (Publicaciones del Instituto de Ciencias Políticas y Administrativas de la Universidad
de Chile)   JL2624.U7

140
Weil, Thomas E., *and others.* Area handbook for Chile. [Washington, U.S. Govt.
Print. Off.] 1969. xiv, 509 p.   F3058.W44
"DA pam. no. 550–77."

CHINA

141
Ch'ien, Tuan-shêng. The government and politics of China, 1912–1949. Stanford,
Calif., Stanford University Press [1970, c1950] xviii, 526 p.   JQ1502.C46 1970

142
China *(National Government of the Republic of China, 1940–1945)* Chung-hua min
kuo min chêng fu kai lan. The National Government of China, organization
and personnel, October 1941. Nanking, Compilation Bureau, International Publicity Board [1941?] [63 p.]   JQ1501.A11 1941 Orien China

143
The China annual. [1943–44?] Shanghai, Asia Statistics Co.   DS706.C49

144
The China year book. 1912–39. Shanghai, North China Daily News & Herald. 20 v.
JQ1501.A16
     No volumes issued for 1915, 1917–18, 1920, 1927, 1933, 1937.

145
China yearbook. 1937/43–[1950?] New York, Rockport Press.   DS701.C6438
     Publication suspended 1947–49? Volumes for 1937/43–1937/45 compiled
     by the Chinese Ministry of Information.

146
Tung, Lin.   The political institutions of modern China. The Hague, M. Nijhoff,
     1964. 408 p.   JQ1502.T8
     Includes both the People's Republic and the Republic of China after 1949.

CHINA, PEOPLE'S REPUBLIC OF

147
Directory of Chinese Communist officials [n.p.] 1971. 434 p. (Reference aid)
JQ1507.D52 1971
     "Identifies Chinese Communist personalities holding positions in the Chi-
     nese Communist Party, revolutionary committees, military organizations, the
     national government, and the diplomatic and consular corps."

148
A Guide to new China. [3d ed.] Peking, Foreign Language Press, 1953. 124 p.
JQ1501.A175 1953

149
Jiang, Joseph.   Chinese bureaucracy and government administration, an annotated
     bibliography. [Honolulu] Research Translations, East-West Center, 1964. 157 l.
     (Occasional papers of the Institute of Advanced Projects. Annotated bibliog-
     raphy series no. 1)   Z7165.C6J5

150
Kondrat'ev, Rem-Sergeevich.   Gosudarstvennyĭ stroĭ Kitaĭskoĭ Narodnoĭ Respubliki.
     Moskva, Gos. izd-vo i͡urid. lit-ry, 1959. 123 p. (Gosudarstvennyĭ stroĭ stran
     mira)   JQ1503 1959.K6

151
Tsien, Tche-hao.   L'Administration en Chine populaire. [Paris] Presses universi-
     taires de France [1973] 94 p. (Dossiers Thémis, 54. Série Systèmes adminis-
     tratifs comparés)   JQ1508.T84

152
U.S. *Consulate General. Hongkong.*   Biographic information; report no. 1+ Hong-
     kong, 1960+   JQ1507.U48
     Includes government officials listed by agency.

153
U.S. *Dept. of the Army.*   Communist China: a bibliographic survey. [Washington,
     U.S. Govt. Print. Off.] 1974. 253 p.   Z3108.A5U48
     Appendix B: Government organization chart.

154
Waller, Derek J. The government and politics of Communist China. Garden City, N.Y., Anchor Books, 1971 [c1970]   JQ1503 1971.W35

155
Whitaker, Donald P., *and others.* Area handbook for the People's Republic of China. [Washington, U.S. Govt. Print. Off.] 1972. xvi, 729 p.   DS706.W46
"DA pam. no. 550–60."

156
Wu, Yuan-li. China: a handbook. New York, Praeger [1973] 915 p. (Handbooks to the modern world)   DS706.W8

CHINA, REPUBLIC OF

157
China yearbook. 1937/43+ Taipeh, China Pub. Co.   DS777.53.C459
    Publication suspended 1947–49? Title varies: 1937/43–1956/57, *China Handbook.* Some volumes compiled by the Chinese Ministry of Information. (See also under China.)

158
Directory of Taiwan. 1951+ [Taipeh, China News & Publication Service]
                    DS895.F7D57

159
Chaffee, Frederic H., *and others.* Area handbook for the Republic of China. [Washington, U.S. Govt. Print. Off.] 1969 [i. e. 1972] xiv. 435 p.   DS895.F9C4
"DA pam. no. 550–63."

160
U.S. *Embassy. China.* List of high-ranking Chinese government officials and Kuomintang leaders. Taipei, American Embassy, 1966. 68 p.   JQ1507.U5

COLOMBIA

161
Colombia. *Secretaría de Organización e Inspección de la Administración Pública.* Manual de organización de la rama ejecutiva del Poder Público. [Bogotá, Impr. Nacional] 1970. xlviii, 341 p.   JL2831.C65 1970
    Earlier edition published in 1961.

162
Bohorquez C., José Ignacio. Lista alfabética de las entidades de la administración pública nacional de Colombia, 1821–1966. *In* Seminar on the Acquisition of Latin American Library Materials, *11th, New York City, 1966.* Final report and working papers. Working paper no. 4.   Z688.L4S38 11th, 1966

163
Weil, Thomas E., *and others.* Area handbook for Colombia. [Washington, U.S. Govt. Print. Off.] 1970. xiv, 595 p.   F2258.W43
"DA pam. no. 550–26."

CONGO, PEOPLE'S REPUBLIC OF THE

164
Gauze, René.   The politics of Congo-Brazzaville. Translation, editing, and supplement by Virginia Thompson and Richard Adloff. Stanford, Calif., Hoover Institution Press, Stanford University [c1973] xxvii, 283 p. (Hoover Institution publication, 129)   DT546.276.G38

165
McDonald, Gordon C., *and others*.   Area handbook for People's Republic of the Congo. [Washington, U.S. Govt. Print. Off.] 1971. 255 p.   DT546.2.M25
"DA pam. no. 550–91."

COSTA RICA

166
Costa Rica. *Oficina de Planificación*.   Manual de organización de la administración pública. San José, 1968. 468 p.
First edition was published in 1962 by the Oficina del Presupuesto, Sección de Organización y Metodos.

167
Associación Costarricense de Bibliotecarios. List of author headings for the principal government offices of Costa Rica. Washington, Pan American Union, 1965. 17 l. (10th SALALM. Working paper no. 15)   Z689.S4 10th, no. 15

168
Blutstein, Howard I., *and others*.   Area handbook for Costa Rica. [Washington, U.S. Govt. Print. Off.] 1970. xiv, 323 p.   F1543.B66
"DA pam. no. 550–90."

CUBA

169
Directory of personalities of the Cuban Government, official organizations, and mass organizations. [n. p.] 1973. 1102 p. (Reference aid)   JL1007.A3 1973

170
Anglo-American directory of Cuba. A.A.D.O.C. Almendares, Marianao, Cuba [1954–60?]   F1754.5.A6

171
Anuario de información fiscal, judicial, social y administrativa. t. 1–? 1942–? Habana, Cuba, Editorial Neptuno.   JL1000.A15A6

172
Blutstein, Howard I., *and others*.   Area handbook for Cuba. [Washington, U.S. Govt. Print. Off.] 1971. 505 p.   F1758.B55
"DA pam. no. 550–152."

173
Directorio de información general de la República de Cuba [1907–8?] Habana, Impr. de Rambla, Bouza y Ca. F1754.5.A

174
Guía de forasteros de la siempre fiel isla de Cuba. Habana, Impr. del Gobierno y Capitania General por S. M. [1817–84?] annual. JL1007.G8

175
Guía-directorio de la República de Cuba. 2. época, año 1–? 1912–? Barcelona, "Anuarios Bailly-Baillière y Riera reunidos." F1754.5.G8

176
Muñoz Bonal, Francisco. Directorio administrativo y judicial de Cuba. Habana, Imprenta Alemana, 1925. 383 p. DLC LL

CYPRUS

177
The Diplomatic Press directory of the Republic of Cyprus, including trade index and biographical section. London, Diplomatic Press and Publishing Co. DS54.A2D5

178
Gt. Brit. *Colonial Office.* Annual report on Cyprus. 1946–[59?] London, H. M. Stationery Off. (*Its* Colonial annual reports) DS54.A2A33

179
A Handbook of Cyprus. [1905–30?] London, E. Stanford. DS54.H2

180
Keefe, Eugene K., *and others.* Area handbook for Cyprus. [Washington, U.S. Govt. Print. Off.] 1971. xiv, 241 p. DS54.K4 1971
"DA pam. no. 550–22."

181
Kyriakides, Stanley. Cyprus: constitutionalism and crisis government. Philadelphia, University of Pennsylvania Press. [1968] 212 p. JQ663 1968.K9

CZECHOSLOVAKIA

182
Czechoslovak Republic. *Československá tisková kancelář, Prague.* Organizace Československé socialistické republiky. Praha, 1965+ 1 v. (looseleaf) JN2217.A53
Organization of the Czechoslovak Socialist Republic.

183
Directory of Czechoslovak officials. [n. p.] 1970. 280 p. JN2217.D5 1970

184
U.S. *Central Intelligence Agency.* Directory of Czechoslovak officials. [1972+ Washington] (Reference aid) JN2217.U55

185
Batovcův almanach; politický kalendář Republiky československé. [1920–?] V Praze,
    Tiskem a nákladem F. B. Batovce.   JN2217.B3
        Batovec's almanac; political calendar of the Czechoslovak Republic. In-
    cludes detailed organization of central government agencies.

186
Bidlo, Bořivoj, Dušan Hendrych, and Aleš Šrámek. Organizace ústřední státní
    správy Československé socialistické republiky. Praha, Ústav státní správy, 1970.
    293 p. (Studie a informace, roč. 4)   JN2220.B5
        Organization of the central state administration.

187
Československá federace. Praha, Ústav státní správy, 1969. 253 [2] p. (Studie a in-
    formace, roč. 3)   DLC LL
        The Czechoslovak federation.

188
Československá federace. Uspoř. Václav Brož, red. slov. části Ol'ga Slušná. Praha,
    ČTK, 1969+   JN2211.A1C4
        The Czechoslovak federation. Contents: 1. State power and administration.
    –2. Production basis I. –3. Production basis II.

189
Czechoslovak Republic. Laws, statutes, etc. Organisace politické správy v Republice
    československé; zákony a nařízení k ní se vztahující. Praha, Nákl. Československé-
    ho kompasu, 1928. 1039 p. (Komentované zákony Československé republiky, sv.
    28)   DLC LL
        Organization of the political administration in the Czechoslovak Republic,
    including pertinent laws and decrees.

190
Hendrych, Dušan, and Aleš Šrámek. Československá státní správa. Praha, Orbis,
    1973. 117 [2] p. (Edice Socialistická státní politika)   JN2220.H46
        The Czechoslovak state administration.

191
Keefe, Eugene K., and others. Area handbook for Czechoslovakia. [Washington,
    U.S. Govt. Print. Off.] 1972. xiv, 321 p.   DB196.K4
    "DA pam. no. 550–158."

192
Kuhn, Heinrich, and others. Handbuch der Tschechoslowakei. [München] Lerche
    [formerly Calve, Prague] 1966. 1021 p. (Veröffentlichungen des Collegiums
    Carolinum)   JN2217.K8
        A handbook of Czechoslovakia. Includes detailed description of govern-
    mental structure.

193
Organisace československého státního zřízení. roč. 1–2, 1946–48. Praha, Orbis.
                                                         JN2220.O7
        Organization of the Czechoslovak state administration.

194
Shavrov, Ĩaroslav M. Gosudarstvennyĭ stroĭ Chekhoslovatskoĭ Respubliki. Moskva,
    Gos. izd-vo ĩurid. lit-ry, 1957. 76 p. (Gosudarstvennyĭ stroĭ stran mira)
                                                         JN2213 1957.S5
        Government organization of the Czechoslovak Republic.

For the government in exile (1939-45), see:

195
Carnegie Endowment for International Peace. *Library.* European governments in
exile. Compiled by Helen N. Scanlon. [Washington, 1943] 24 p. (*Its* Memoranda series, no. 3. Revised January 25, 1943) JX1906.A35 no. 3a
Published originally in 1942. Czechoslovakia: p. 4-6.

196
Czechoslovak Republic. Úřední věstník československý. [1940-45] V Londýně.
  J7.A913
Official gazette. January-May 1940 published in Paris.

DAHOMEY

197
Dahomey. *Secrétariat d'État à l'information.* Dahomey; un an d'indépendence,
1ᵉʳ août 1960-1ᵉʳ août 1961. [Porto-Novo? 1961] 116 p. DT541.8.A47

198
Dahomey. *Service de l'information.* Republic of Dahomey. Porto-Novo, Management of Information, 1963. 111 l. DT 541.8.A5

199
Glelé, Maurice A. La République du Dahomey. Paris, Berger-Levrault, 1969. 76 p.
(Encyclopédie politique et constitutionnelle. Série Afrique) JQ3376.A3 1969.G55

DENMARK

200
Denmark. Kongelig dansk hof- og statskalender, statshaandbog for kongeriget
Danmark. [1734]+ København. JN7104
Royal Danish court and state calendar and handbook.

201
Denmark. *Rigsarkivet.* Den civile centraladministration, 1914-35. København, Levin
& Munksgaard, 1936. 210 p. JN7191.A5 1936
Earlier editions published for 1848-93 and 1894-1913.

202
Meyer, Poul. Offentlig forvaltning. København, Nyt Nordisk Forlag, 1970. 265 p.
  JF1358.D36M37
Public administration.

DOMINICAN REPUBLIC

203
Dominican Republic. *Oficina Nacional de Administración y Personal.* Manual de
organización del gobierno. [Santo Domingo, 1969] 1 v. (various pagings) (*Its*
Publicaciones, 8) JL1132.B3 vol. 8

204
Arzeno, Julio. Los gobiernos y administraciones de Santo Domingo (nómina sucinta) 1492–1934. Puerto Plata, Tipografía "El Diario," 1931. 57, [3] p.   JL1122.A9

205
Weil, Thomas E., *and others.* Area handbook for the Dominican Republic. Washington, U.S. Govt. Print. Off., 1973. 261 p.   F1934.W44
    "DA pam. no. 550–54."

206
Wiarda, Howard J. Materials for the study of politics and government in the Dominican Republic, 1930–1966. [Edición en inglés y español. Santiago de los Caballeros] UCMM [1968] 142 p. (Universidad Católica Madre y Maestra. Collección estudios, 5)   Z7165.D6W5

ECUADOR

207
Quito. Universidad Central. *Instituto de Estudios Administrativos.* Manual de gobierno, República del Ecuador. [Quito, Editorial Universitaria, 1965] 445 p.
                          JL3031.Q5 1965
————— ————— Indice de organigramas. [Quito, Editorial Universitaria, cover 1965. 3 p.]   JL3031.Q5 Index
    Compiled in collaboration with U.S. Agency for International Development. First edition published in 1962.

208
Compañia "Guía del Ecuador." El Ecuador, guía comercial, agricola, e industrial. Guayaquil, E. Rodenas, 1909. 1,328 p.   F3708.C73
    An earlier edition published in 1906. Includes governmental organization.

209
Directorio general de la República Ecuador. [1928–?] Quito, Talleres de la Escuela de Artes y Oficios.   F3708.D65

210
Weil, Thomas E., *and others.* Area handbook for Ecuador. [Washington, U.S. Govt. Print. Off.] 1973. 403 p.   F3708.W44
    "DA pam. no. 550–52."

EGYPT, ARAB REPUBLIC OF [1958–71: UNITED ARAB REPUBLIC]

211
Dadiani, Lionel' ĪA. Gosudarstvennyĭ stroĭ Ob'edinennoĭ Arabskoĭ Respubliki. Moskva, ĪUrid. lit-ra, 1967. 109 p.   JQ3815 1956.D3
    Governmental organization of the United Arab Republic.

212
Directory of U.A.R. personnages. [Cairo, 1963–64?]   JQ3821.D5
    Prepared by the Press Analysis Office, Political Section, U.S. Embassy, Cairo.

213
Egypt. *Government Press.* Almanac. 1902–? Cairo.   DT43.A3
    From 1940, only supplements published giving no information on governmental organization.

214
The Egyptian directory of the United Arab Republic. L'Annuaire égyptien du commerce et de l'industrie. Le Caire. annual. DT44.E4
Began publication in 1887, ceased 1964? From 1917, also in Arabic: *al-Dalīl al-Miṣrī lil-Jumhūrīyah al-ʿArabīyah al-Muttahidah* (DT44.D3 Orien Arab).

215
Gulick, Luther H., *and* James K. Pollock. Government reorganization in the U. A. R. A report submitted to the Central Committee for the Reorganization of the Machinery of Government. Cairo, 1962. 171 p. JQ3840.G82
Title of the Arabic edition: *Tanẓīm al-adāh al-ḥukūmyīah fī al-Jumhūrīyah al-ʿArabīyah al-Muttaḥidah* (JQ3831.G8412 Orien Arab).

216
Smith, Harvey H., *and others*. Area handbook for the United Arab Republic (Egypt). [Washington, U.S. Govt. Print. Off.] 1970. xx, 555 p.
DT107.83.S59 1970
"DA pam. no. 550–43."

217
Who's who in U. A. R. and the Near East. [1935–59?] Cairo. annual. DT44.W47

EL SALVADOR

218
Guía de instituciones del Estado. [1969?]+ San Salvador, Secretaría de Información de la Presidencia de la República. JL1567.A2A3

———

219
Alvarado, Hermógenes. Organización administrativa de la República de El Salvador. San Salvador, Imprenta Nacional, 1918. 151 [2] p. JL1570.A6

220
Blutstein, Howard I., *and others*. Area handbook for El Salvador. [Washington, U.S. Govt. Print. Off.] 1971. 259 p. HN183.5.B55
"DA pam. no. 550–150."

221
Poder ejecutivo de la República de El Salvador; composición ministerio y sus instituciones autonomas. San Salvador, Dirección General de Estadística y Censos, 1962.

222
Public Administration Service. Informe sobre la conveniencia de introducir mejoras en la organización del Gobernio de El Salvador. Chicago [1950] 81 l.
JL1570.P8 1950

ETHIOPIA

223
Addis Ababa. Imperial Ethiopian Institute of Public Administration. Administrative directory of the Imperial Ethiopian Government. [1957?]+ Addis Ababa.
JQ3757.A6

224
Clapham, Christopher S. Haile-Selassie's government. Harlow, Longmans, 1969.
xiv. 218 p.   JQ3760.C4 1969

225
Ethiopia. *Ministry of Information.* Government in Ethiopia. Addis Ababa, Pub-
lications & Foreign Languages Press Dept., Ministry of Information, 1966. 44 p.
(Patterns of Progress, book 7)   JQ3753 1966.A55

226
Howard, William E. H. Public administration in Ethiopia; a study in retrospect
and prospect. Groningen, J. B. Wolters, 1955. 204 p.   JQ3754.H6

227
Kaplan, Irving, *and others.* Area handbook for Ethiopia. [Washington, U.S. Govt.
Print. Off.] 1971. xiv, 543 p.   DT373.K33 1971
"DA pam. no. 550–28."

228
Keussler, Klaus M. von. Das Verwaltungssystem im Kaiserrreich Äthiopien nach
dem Stand von 1966/67. Berlin, 1967. 19 p. (Deutsche Stiftung für Entwick-
lungsländer. Zentralstelle für öffentliche Verwaltung, Dok. 431)
HC59.7.D385 no. 431

229
Leclercq, Claude. L'empire d'Éthiopie. Paris, Berger-Levrault, 1969. 80 p. (Encyclopédie politique et constitutionnelle. Série Afrique)   JQ3753 1969.L4

230
Perham, *Dame* Margery F. The government of Ethiopia. [New ed.] Evanston,
Northwestern University Press, 1969. xci, 531 p.   JQ3754.P4 1969b

FIJI

231
Fiji. Civil list. [1940?]+ Suva.   JQ6301.A3

232
Gt. Brit. *Colonial Office.* Annual report on Fiji. [1947–70]   DU600.A33

233
Henderson, John W., *and others.* Area handbook for Oceania. [Washington,
U.S. Govt. Print. Off.] 1971. xiv, 555 p.   DU17.H45
"DA pam. no. 550–94."
Fiji: p. 204–212.

234
Tudor, Judy, *ed.* Handbook of Fiji. 2d ed. Sydney, Pacific Publications Pty., 1965.
272 p.   DU600.T8 1965

FINLAND

235
Suomen valtiokalenteri . . . julkaisut Helsingin yliopisto. Helsinki.   JN6707
Finnish government directory, published since 1869. A Swedish edition,
Finlands statskalender, published since 1811.

236
Finland. *Unesco Toimikunta.* Luettelo Suomen virastojen ja julkisten laitosten englannin-, ranskan-, saksan-, ja venäjänkielisistä nimistä. Förteckning över engelska, franska, tyska och ryska benämningar på ämbetsverk och offentliga inrättningar i Finland. Helsinki, 1962. 59 p. JN6701.A17
List of names of government agencies and institutions in English, French German, and Russian.

237
Julkunen, Martti, *and* Anja Lehikoinen. A select list of books and articles in English, French, and German on Finnish politics in the 19th and 20th century. Turku, Institute of Political History, University of Turku, 1967. 125 p. (Institute of Political History, University of Turku [Publication] B:1) Z2520.J8

238
Nousiainen, Jaakko. The Finnish political system. Translated by John H. Hodgson. Cambridge, Mass., Harvard University Press, 1971. 454 p. JN6703 1959.N613

239
Popov, Dmitriĭ I. Gosudarstvennyĭ stroĭ Finliandii. Moskva, Gos. izd-vo iurid. lit-ry, 1958. 57 p. (Gosudarstvennyĭ stroĭ stran mira) JU6703 1958.P6

FRANCE

240
Bottin administratif et documentaire. 1942+ Paris, Société Didot-Bottin. annual.
JN2303.B6

241
France. *Secrétariat général du gouvernement.* Composition du gouvernement et des cabinets ministériels. [Paris] Documentation française [1950?]+ irregular.
JN2304.S4

242
Répertoire permanent de l'administration française. 15 fév. 1945+ Paris, Centre national d'information économique. irregular. JN2304 date p

---

243
Annuaire d'adresses des fonctionnaires des Ministères des travaux publics, de la marine marchande, de l'air, du commerce et de l'industrie, des services, associations, syndicats et sociétés industrielles qui s'y rattachent. [1875–39?] Paris, Bureau des huissiers du Cabinet du Ministre des travaux publics. JN2304 date b
"Cet annuaire a été fondé en 1875."

244
L'Annuaire des ministères. Paris. JN2304 date c
Began publication with issue for 1936?; suspended 1941?–44. Supplements published in 1945 and 1946, later issued monthly and called *Revue de l'administration française, Annuaire des ministères.* From 1949 to 1965, same publisher issued *Encyclopédie permanente de l'administration française* (see below). The *Annuaire des ministères* ceased publication in 1964?

245
Annuaire général. [1.–10?] année; [1919–28?] Paris, Larousse. DC1.A5
Title 1919–26: *Annuaire général de la France et de l'étranger.*

246
Annuaire général du commerce et de l'industrie, de la magistrature et de l'administration. [1838–57] Paris, Firmin Didot Frères.   DC15.A5
    In 1857 absorbed by *Bottin* (see below).

246a
Baecque, Francis de. L'Administration centrale de la France. Paris, A. Colin
    [1973] 398 p. (Collection U. Série Droit public interne)   JN2728.B3

247
Bajot, Louis M.   Chronologie ministérielle de trois siècles; ou, Liste nominative par
    ordre chronologique de tous les ministres de la justice, des affaires étrangères,
    de la guerre, de la marine, des finances, de l'intérieur, du commerce, de la police
    générale, des cultes, et de l'instruction publique . . . précédé d'un tableau des
    gouvernements depuis 1515 jusqu'en 1844. 4. éd. Paris, Imprimerie royale,
    1844. 83 p.   JN2681.B2

248
Bottin. [1797?+   ] Paris, Annuaire du commerce Didot-Bottin.   HF53.B6
    Title varies. Until 1942, when *Bottin administratif et documentaire* started
    publication, it included in its "Paris" volume a detailed listing of govern-
    ment agencies.

249
Centre national d'organisation scientifique du travail. Guide administratif des services
    ministériels français actuellement à Paris. Juin 1941. [Paris] Librairies-Impri-
    meries réunis [1941] 105 p.   JN2737.C4
    Contains list of branches of Vichy government agencies located in Paris
    under German occupation.

250
Echeman, Jacques.   Les ministères en France de 1914 à 1932. Paris, Marcel Rivière,
    1932. 98 p.   JN2681.E25

251
Encyclopédie permanente de l'administration française. no. 1–[491?] juin 1949–
    [mai/juin 1965] Paris.   JN2301.E53
    A looseleaf monthly (irregular) publication listing changes in the French
    government and including other documentary material. (See also *L'Annuaire
    des ministères* above.)

252
France. Almanach national. Paris.   JN2304
    Since 1700, the official almanac of France, until 1919. Title varies:
    Almanach royal (1700–1792); *Almanach national de France* (1793–1804);
    Almanach royal (1805); *Almanach impérial* (1806–14); *Almanach royal*
    (1814–30); *Almanach royal et national* (1831–47); *Almanach national. An-
    nuaire de la République Française* (1848–52); *Almanach impérial* (1853–70);
    Almanach national, annuaire officiel de la République Française (1872–1919).
    Continuation of *Almanac ou calendrier pour l'an 1683–[1699]*.

253
Saffroy, Gaston.   Bibliographie des almanachs et annuaires administratifs, ecclésias-
    tiques et militaires français de l'ancien régime; et des almanachs et annuaires
    généalogiques et nobiliaires du xvie siècle à nos jours. Paris, Librairie G. Saffroy,
    1959. xvi, 109 p.   Z2174.A54S32

254
U.S. *Office of Strategic Services. Research and Analysis Branch.* A selected who's
who in Vichy, France, June 1940–August 1944. [Washington] 1944. 358 p. (*Its*
R & A no. 2344) UB250.U33 no. 2344

For the organization of the Free French Government (France combattante), during the Second World War, the following works will be of
assistance:

255
[Boillot, Félix F.] The three years of fighting France, June 1940–June 1943, by
Félix de Grand' Combe [*pseud.*] London, Wells Gardner, Darton & Co. [1943]
201, [2] p. D761.9.F7B6

256
Carnegie Endowment for International Peace. *Library.* European governments in
exile. Compiled by Helen L. Scanlon. [Washington, 1943] 24 p. (*Its* Memoranda
series no. 3. Revised January 25, 1943) JX1906.A35 no. 3a
Originally issued in 1942. French National Committee: p. 7–9.

257
Fighting French year book. 1942–45. New York, France Forever. 4 v. in 1.
D761.9.F7F5

258
France combattante. Journal officiel. 20 jan. 1941–10 août 1943. [Londres, 1941–43]
3 v. monthly (irregular) D761.9.F7F672

259
La France continue la lutte, textes et documents, 1940–1943. [Paris? 1943] 125 p.
D761.9.F7F6729

260
Silvère, Jean. Le gouvernement français à Alger, 1943–1944. Alger [Ancienne
imprimerie V. Heintz, 1944] 63 [1] p. D761.9.F7S5

GABON

261
Annuaire national officiel de la République gabonaise. 1973+ [Libreville, Agence
Havas Gabon] JQ3407.A1A5

262
Gabon. *Direction de l'information.* Réalités gabonaises. [Paris, Éditions Diloutremer,
1960] 187 p. JQ3407.A63A5
Includes list of executive departments.

GAMBIA

263
Gambia. Civil list. Bathurst. JQ3001.A4
Since 1968 called *Staff List.*

264
Gt. Brit. *Colonial Office.* Annual report on the Gambia. 1946–[62/63?] London,
    H. M. Stationery Off. (*Its* Colonial annual reports)   DT509.A33
    Biennial from 1950/51.

GERMANY (before 1945)

265
Germany. *Reichsministerium des Innern.* Handbuch für das Deutsche Reich. [1.]–46.
    Jahrg.; 1874–1936. Berlin, C. Heymann. 46 v.   JN3204
    Superseded in 1953 by *Handbuch für die Bundesrepublik Deutschland,*
    which was absorbed from 1956/57 by *Die Bundesrepublik Deutschland* (see
    this under Germany, Federal Republic of).

266
Kürschner's Staats-, Hof- und Kommunal-Handbuch des Reichs und der Einzel-
    Staaten, zugleich Statistisches Jahrbuch. Leipzig, G. J. Göschensche Verlags-
    handlung [1901–07]   JN3203

267
Münz, Ludwig.   Führer durch die Behörden und Organisationen. Berlin, Duncker &
    Humblot, 1939. 466 (i.e. 468) p.   JN3203 1939.M8
    Issued previously in 1933, 1934, and 1936.

268
Prussia. Handbuch über den königlich preussischen Hof und Staat [1889–1913]
    Berlin.   JN4424

GERMANY, DEMOCRATIC REPUBLIC

269
Jahrbuch der Deutschen Demokratischen Republik. 1.+ 1956+ Berlin.   DD261.J3
    Published by Deutsches Institut für Zeitgeschichte.

270
Bonn. *Archiv für Gesamtdeutsche Fragen.* Der Staatsapparat der "Deutschen De-
    mokratischen Republik." Bonn, 1969. 42 p.   JN3971.5.A4B6 1969
    First edition published in 1966.

271
Directory of East German officials. [n. p.] 1970. 301 p.   DD261.63.D52
    Published in 1964 and 1967 also.

272
Germany (*Democratic Republic, 1949–*) *Volkskammer.* Die Volkskammer der
    Deutschen Demokratischen Republik. 1957+ Berlin, Staatsverlag.
                                                                JN3971.5.A7A35
    Handbook of the East German Parliament. Includes list of government
    agencies.

273
Gesamtdeutsches Institut.   Staats- und Parteiapparat der DDR; personelle Besetzung.
    [15. Jan. 1972]+ [Bonn]   JN3971.5.A4G47

274
Hoffmann, Ursula. Die Veränderungen in der Sozialstruktur des Ministerrates der
    DDR 1949–1969. Düsseldorf, Droste Verlag [c1971] 114 p. (Mannheimer
    Schriften zur Politik und Zeitgeschichte, 1)   JN3971.5.A63H64

275
Keefe, Eugene K., *and others.* Area handbook for East Germany. [Washington, U.S.
    Govt. Print. Off.] 1972. xiv, 329 p.   DD261.K4
    "DA pam. no. 550–155."

276
Der Staatsapparat der Deutschen Demokratischen Republik. 5. Aufl. Stand: Dez.
    1970. Bonn, Gesamtdeutsches Institut, Bundesanstalt für gesamtdeutsche Auf-
    gaben, 1971. 51 p.   JN3971.5.A4S7 1971
    First four editions published by Archiv für gesamtdeutsche Fragen, Bonn
    (see above).

277
Ur'îâs, Îûriĭ P. Gosudarstvennyĭ stroĭ Germanskoĭ Demokraticheskoĭ Respubliki.
    Moskva, Gos. izd-vo îûrid. lit-ry, 1957 79 p. (Gosudarstvennyĭ stroĭ stran mira)
                                                        JN3971.5.A3 1957a

GERMANY, FEDERAL REPUBLIC OF

278
Ämter und Organisationen der Bundesrepublik Deutschland. Frankfurt/Main.
                                                    JN3971.A125A62 no. 1+
    Some 43 volumes have been published in this series since 1966, each volume
    dealing with an individual government agency.

279
Die Bundesrepublik Deutschland. Köln, C. Heymann.   JN3971.A485
    Began in 1889 as *Taschen-Kalender für Beamte* (title varies), 1953–62/63,
    called *Die Bundesrepublik.* Suspended 1944–49.

280
American University, *Washington, D.C. Foreign Areas Studies Division.* Area hand-
    book for Germany. 2d ed. [Washington] Headquarters, Dept. of the Army,
    1964. 955 p.   DD61.A495 1964
    "DA pam. no. 550–29."

281
Deutschland im Wiederaufbau; Tätigkeitsbericht der Bundesregierung. 1950–[1966]
    Bonn.   JN3971.A2D4
    For 1960–66 called *Deutsche Politik.* Since 1967 called *Jahresbericht der
    Bundesregierung* (see below).

282
Germany (*Federal Republic, 1949–*) *Bundesregierung.* Jahresbericht. [1967+
    Bonn]   JN3971.A1G42a
    Continues *Deutsche Politik.*

283
Germany *(Federal Republic, 1949–   ) Bundesministerium des Innern.* Handbuch
    für die Bundesrepublik Deutschland. 1953–54. Köln, C. Heymann. 2 v.
                                                                    JN3971.A42
        Superseded *Handbuch für das Deutsche Reich,* issued 1874–1936. In 1956/
    57 absorbed by *Die Bundesrepublik.*

GHANA   [before 1957: GOLD COAST]

284
Ghana, an official handbook, 1961–? [Accra, Ministry of Information and Broad-
    casting] annual.   JQ3021.A11A3

285
Ghana official handbook. [1968?+ Accra, Ghana Information Services]
                                                                   DT510.2.A3

286
Ghana year book. [1953+ Accra]   DT511.A17
    "A Daily Graphic publication."
    Earlier called *Gold Coast Year Book.*

———————

287
Ghana. *National Assembly.* List of ministers, ministerial secretaries, members, and
    principal officers and officials. [Accra-Tema, Ghana Pub. Corp.] 1971. 12 p.
                                                                   JQ3027.A54

288
Goldman, Dietrich.   Ghana, Staatsverwaltung und Stammesstruktur; eine Analyse
    des ghanesischen Verwaltungsaufbaus seit 1874. Köln, Heymann [1971] xxxxiii,
    260 p. (Schriften zur Verwaltungslehre, Heft 10)   JQ3023 1971.G65
    A study of the development of government structure in Ghana.

289
Gt. Brit. *Colonial Office.*   Annual report on the Gold Coast. 1946–[54?] London,
    H. M. Stationery Off. (*Its* Colonial annual reports)   DT511.A323

290
Kaplan, Irving, *and others.*   Area handbook for Ghana. Rev. 2d ed. [Washington,
    U.S. Govt. Print. Off.] 1971. xiv, 449 p.   DT510.K37   1971
    "DA pam. no. 550–153."

GREAT BRITAIN

291
Britain; an official handbook. [1949/50]+ London, H. M. Stationery Off. annual.
                                                                   DA630.A17
    Issued by the Central Office of Information.

292
The British imperial calendar and civil service list. [1809]+ London [H. M. Sta-
    tionery Off.] annual.   JN106.B8
        Prepared by the Treasury. In 1974 called *Civil Service Yearbook,* prepared
    by the Civil Service Department.

293
Gt. Brit. *Treasury. Organisation and Methods Division.* Historical table of changes
in government organisation. [London] 1957. 81 p.   JN123.G7

294
Royal Institute of Public Administration. The organisation of British central government 1914–1964: a survey by a group of the Royal Institute of Public Administration; edited by D. N. Chester; written by F. M. G. Willson. 2d ed. London,
Allen & Unwin, 1968. 521 p.   JN425.R67 1968

295
The New Whitehall series, prepared under the auspices of the Royal Institute of
Public Administration, and published by George Allen & Unwin, London, and
Oxford University Press, New York, since 1954, included the following works:

1. Newsam, *Sir* Frank.   The Home Office. (1954. 224 p. JN453.H7N4)
2. Strang, William S., *Baron.*   The Foreign Office. (1955. 226 p. JX1783.S8)
3. Jeffries, *Sir* Charles J.   The Colonial Office. (1956. 222 p. JV1043.J4)
4. Emmerson, *Sir* Harold.   The Ministry of Works. (1956. 171 p. HD4147.E5)
5. Milne, *Sir* David.   The Scottish Office and other Scottish Government departments. (1957. 232 p. JN1228.M5)
6. King, *Sir* Geoffrey S.   The Ministry of Pensions and National Insurance. (1958.
   162 p. HD7167.K5)
7. Jenkins, *Sir* Gilmour.   The Ministry of Transport and Civil Aviation. (1959.
   231 p. HE243.J4)
8. Ince, *Sir* Godfrey H.   The Ministry of Labour and National Service. (1960.
   215 p. HD4835.G7I6)
9. Melville, *Sir* Harry W.   The Department of Scientific and Industrial Research.
   (1962. 200 p. Q180.G7M4)
10. Crombie, *Sir* James.   Her Majesty's Customs and Excise. (1962. 224 p.
    HJ6891.A8 1962)
11. Winnifrith, *Sir* John.   The Ministry of Agriculture, Fisheries and Food. (1962.
    271 p. S217.W5)
12. Bridges, Edward E. B., *Baron.*   The Treasury. 2d. ed. (1966. 248 p. HJ1030.B68
    1966)
13. Johnston, *Sir* Alexander.   The Inland Revenue. (1965. 201 p. HJ5118.J58)
14. Sharp, Evelyn, *Baroness.*   The Ministry of Housing and Local Government.
    (1969. 253 p.)
15. Clark, *Sir* Fife.   The Central Office of Information. (1970. 184 p. JN329.P8C6)

GREECE

296
Hōdēgos dēmosiōn hyperēsiōn kai organismōn dēmosiou kai idiōtikou dikaiou. 1+
1960+ Athēnai, Hellēnikos Organismos Dēmosiōn Scheseōn "Horizōn."
                JN5060.A1H6
   Guide to official organizations in Greece.

297
Carnegie Endowment for International Peace. *Library.* European governments in
exile. Compiled by Helen L. Scanlon. [Washington, 1943] 24 p. (*Its* Memoranda
series, no. 3. Revised January 25, 1943)   JX1906.A35 no. 3a
   Originally published in 1942. Greece: p. 10–11.

298
Herrick, Allison B., *and others.* Area handbook for Greece. [Washington, U.S.
Govt. Print. Off.] 1970 [i.e. 1972] xiv, 357 p.   DF717.H44
"DA pam. no. 550–87."

GUATEMALA

299
Dombrowski, John, *and others.* Area handbook for Guatemala. Washington, U.S.
Govt. Print. Off., 1970. xiv, 361 p.   F1463.D65
"DA pam. no. 550–78."

300
Guatemala. *Centro para el Desarrollo de la Administración Pública.* Manual de
organización del gobierno de la República de Guatemala. Marzo 1962. [Guate-
mala, 1962] 70 p.
Prepared by Antonio Monroy of the Division of Public Administration,
U.S. Agency for International Development Mission in Guatemala.

GUINEA

301
Charles, Bernard. La République de Guinée. Paris, Berger-Levrault, 1972. 69 p.
(Encyclopédie politique et constitutionnelle. Série Afrique)
JQ3381.A3 1972.C45

GUYANA

302
Gt. Brit. *Colonial Office.* Annual report on British Guiana. 1946–[61?] London,
H. M. Stationery Off. (*Its* Colonial annual reports)   F2368.G75

303
Johnson Research Associates. Area handbook for Guyana. [Coauthors: William B.
Mitchell and others. Prepared for the American University. Washington, U.S.
Govt. Print. Off.] 1969. xiv, 378 p.   F2368.J6
"DA pam. no. 550–82."

HAITI

304
Weil, Thomas E., *and others.* Area handbook for Haiti. [Washington, U.S. Govt.
Print. Off.] 1973. xiv, 189 p.   F1915.W44
"DA pam. no. 550–164."

HONDURAS

305
Blutstein, Howard I., *and others.* Area handbook for Honduras. [Washington, U.S.
Govt. Print. Off.] 1971. xiv, 225 p.   HN153.5.B56
"DA pam. no. 550–151."

HUNGARY

306
Barabashev, Georgiĭ V. Gosudarstvennyĭ stroĭ Vengerskoĭ Narodnoĭ Respubliki.
Moskva, Gos. izd-vo fûrid. lit-ry, 1961. 91 p. (Gosudarstvennyĭ stroĭ stran mira)
JN2066.B3

307
Besnyö, Károly. Államigazgatási kézikönyv. Böv. teljesen átdolg. kiad. Budapest,
Közgazdasági és Jogi Könyvkiadó, 1966. 546 p. JN2052 1966.B4
Manual on public administration. Enlarged and revised edition. An alpha-
betically arranged handbook of definitions. A new edition issued in 1973.

308
A Demokratikus közigazgatas kézikönyvei. 1.–5. Budapest, Székesfövárosi Irodalmi
és Müvészeti Intézet [1946–47] 5 v. JN2069.D45
Handbooks on public administration.

309
Directory of Hungarian officials. [n. p.] 1964. 141 p. (Biographic reference aid,
BA64–16) DB904.D5

310
Hungary. 1966+ [Budapest] Pannonia Press. annual. DB901.A2

311
Hungary. Központi Statisztikai Hivatal. Magyarország tiszti cím- és névtára. Budapest [1873–1943?] JN2051.A4
From 1873 to 1886 irregular, then annual. Not published 1919–26, 1930,
1933–34. A register of government officials, arranged by agencies.

312
Keefe, Eugene K., *and others.* Area handbook for Hungary. [Washington, U.S.
Govt. Print. Off.] 1973. xiv, 339 p. DB906.K36
"DA pam. no. 550–165."

ICELAND

313
Directory of Iceland. [1st] + ed.; 1907+ Reykjavík, Árbók Íslands. HF3653.I75

314
Agnar Klemens Jónsson. Stjórnarráð Íslands 1904–1964. Reykjavík Sögufélað,
1969. 2 v. (1046 p.) DL335.A65
Governments of Iceland. Appendix lists names of cabinet members and
government officials. A list of selected government publications is also included.

315
Nordal, Jóhannes, *and* Valdimar Kristinsson. Iceland 1966; handbook. Reykjavík,
Central Bank of Iceland, 1967. 390 p. DL313.T52

316
Pokhlebkin, Vil'fâm V. Gosudarstvennyĭ stroĭ Islandii. Moskva fÛrid. lit-ra, 1967.
46 p. JN7382.P6

INDIA

317
All-India civil list; a complete directory of the Indian civil and administrative services
and other higher services under the union and the state governments. [1950?]+
Bombay, Published under the authority of the Govt. of India by the Associated
Advertisers & Printers. semiannual.   JQ221.A63

318
Delhi official directory. [1947]+ New Delhi, President's Secretariat.   JQ221.D4

319
India *(Republic) Ministry of Home Affairs.*   The civil list of Indian administrative
service. [1963?]+ [New Delhi]   JQ221.A298
        Superseded in part the Ministry's *The Civil List; Indian Administrative
Service and Indian Police Service* (see below).

320
———— Official directory. [Jan. 1972]+ New Delhi. [quarterly?]   JQ221.A315

321
The Times of India directory and year book including who's who. 1914+ Bombay,
Bennett, Coleman.   DS405.I7

322
Bhambhri, Chandra P.   Bureaucracy and politics in India. Delhi, Vikas Publications
    [1971] 349 p.   JQ231.B45

323
The Combined civil list for India. [1923–48/49?] Allahabad, Pioneer Press.
                                                                  JQ221 date a

324
Delhi. *Secretariat Training School.* Organisational set-up and functions of the
ministries/departments of the Government of India. 4th ed. New Delhi [1969]
376, 3 p.   JQ242.D4 1969

325
India *(Republic) Ministry of Home Affairs.*   The civil list; Indian administrative
service and Indian police service. Jan. 1, 1956–[61?] Delhi, Manager of
Publications.   JQ221.A294

326
India *(Republic) Organisation and Methods Division.*   Administrative directory of
government of India. [1941–58? New Delhi]   JQ221.A32
327
The India office and Burma office list. [1803–1947] London, Harrison.   JQ202.A3

328
Indian Institute of Public Administration.   The organisation of the government of
India. London, Asia Pub. House [c1958] 416 p.   JQ218.I5

329
Shinn, Rinn-Sup, *and others.*   Area handbook for India. [Washington, U.S. Govt.
Print. Off.] 1970. xx, 791 p.   DS407.S46 1970
    "DA pam. no. 550–21."

INDONESIA [before 1945: DUTCH EAST INDIES]

330
Almanak negara R. I. 1970+ [Djakarta] Menteri Negara Penjempurnaan dan Pembersihan Aparatur Negara Republik Indonesia.   JQ767.A352 Orien Indo
   Superseded *Almanak organisasi negara Republik Indonesia,* issued 1960–?
   by Lembaga Administrasi Negara (JQ767.A35 Orien Indo).
   Government organization manual.

331
Daftar alamat dan nomor telepon pedjabat-pedjabat negara. [1971?+ Djakarta]
   Departemen Penerangan R. I.   JQ767.D33 Orien Indo
   Directory of government officials.

332
Henderson, John W., *and others.* Area handbook for Indonesia. Washington, U.S.
   Govt. Print. Off., 1970. xviii, 569 p.   DS615.H44 1970
   "DA pam. no. 550–39."

333
Indonesia handbook. 1970+ [Djakarta] Dept. of Information, Republic of Indonesia.
   annual.   DS611.A337

334
Kabinet Pembangunan Republik Indonesia, beserta daftar alamat pedjabat Pemerintah
   Republik Indonesia. Tjet. 1. Djakarta, Badan Penerbit Almanak Djakarta/
   Pentja, 1972. 164 p.   JQ767.K25 Orien Indo
   Directory of government officials.

335
Netherlands *(Kingdom, 1815–) Regeeringsvoorlichtingsdienst, Djakarta.* Personalia van staatkundige eenheden (regering en volksvertegenwoordiging) in Indonesiä. Batavia, 1949. 62 p.   JQ767.A52
   Personnel of government agencies (parliament as well) in Indonesia.

336
Regeringsalmanak voor Nederlandsch-Indië. [1820–1942?] Batavia.   JQ761.A11
   Government organization manual for Dutch Indies.

IRAN

337
Iran almanac and book of facts. 1st+ ed.; 1961+ Tehran, Echo of Iran. annual.
        AY1185.I7

___

338
Gable, Richard W. Government and administration in Iran. [Los Angeles] School
   of Public Administration, University of Southern California, 1959. 198 l.
        JQ1785.G3

339
Smith, Harvey H., *and others.* Area handbook for Iran. [Washington, U.S. Govt.
   Print. Off.] 1971. xxii, 653 p.   DS254.5.A63 1971
   "DA pam. no. 550–68."

IRAQ

340
Dalīl al-Jumhūrīyah al-'Irāqīyah. Baghdad, 1961. 824 p.   DS67.8.D3 Orien Arab
      Directory of the Republic of Iraq for 1960.

341
Gt. Brit. *Colonial Office.* Report by His Britannic Majesty's government to the
      Council of the League of Nations on the administration of Iraq. [Oct. 1920–
      Oct. 1932] London.   J693.I7

342
al-Hasanī, 'Abd al-Razzāq, *ed.* al-Uṣūl al-rasmīyah li-tārīkh al-wizārāt al-'Irāqīyah.
      Sidon, Lebanon, 'Irfan Press, 1964. 332 p.   JQ1825.I7H36 Orien Arab
      Official sources for the history of Iraqi cabinets during the monarchy.

343
Iraq. The 'Iraq government list. [1921?–?] Baghdad, Printed at the Govt. Press.
                                                                      JQ1825.I7A3

344
The Iraq directory; a general and commercial directory of Iraq. 1st–? 1936–?
      Baghdad, Dangoor's Printing and Publishing House   DS78.A5I7
            The 1936 edition includes Iraqi cabinets for 1920–35 (p. 87–95), as well
      as legislative and executive departments (p. 115–680).

345
Smith, Harvey H., *and others.* Area handbook for Iraq. Washington, U.S. Govt.
      Print. Off., 1969. xvi, 411 p.   DS70.6.S6
      "DA pam. no. 550–31."
      Revised edition issued in 1971.

IRELAND

346
Eolaí ar sheirbhísí stáit. Directory of state services. [1969+] Dublin, Stationery Off.
                                                                      JN1401.A3

347
Institute of Public Administration, *Dublin.* Administration yearbook and diary.
      1967?+ Dublin.   DLC

348
Irish parliamentary handbook. 1939–? Dublin. Stationery Off.   JN1400.I7

349
Meghen, P. J. A short history of the public service in Ireland. Dublin, Institute of
      Public Administration, 1962. 48 p.   JN1448.M4

350
O'Donnell, James D. How Ireland is governed. Dublin, Foras Riaracháin, Institute
      of Public Administration, 1965. 166 p.   JN1415.O4

351
Thom's directory of Ireland. 1844+ Dublin.   DA979.5.T56

352
Thom's directory of Ireland: Professional directory. 116th+ 1960+ Dublin.
DA979.5.T57
Supersedes, in part, *Thom's Directory of Ireland* and continues its numbering.

ISRAEL

353
Israel. Government yearbook. 1950+ Jerusalem.   J693.P22213

354
Israel. Shenaton ha-memshalah. [1949+ Tel Aviv]   J693.P222 Hebr.
Government yearbook.

355
Badi, Joseph. The government of the State of Israel: a critical account of its parliament, executive, and judiciary. New York, Twayne Publishers [c1963] 307 p.   JQ1825.P3B2

356
Gt. Brit. *Colonial Office.* Report by His Majesty's government . . . to the council of the League of Nations on the administration of Palestine and Trans-Jordan. 1920/21–[47?] London, H. M. Stationery Off.   J693.P22

357
Luke, *Sir* Harry Ch. J., *and* Edward Keith-Roach. The handbook of Palestine and Trans-Jordan. 3d ed. London, Macmillan and Co., 1934. xvi, 549 p.
DS107.3.L8 1934
First edition, 1922; second edition, 1930.
"Issued under the authority of the government of Palestine."

358
Smith, Harvey H., *and others.* Area handbook for Israel. [Washington, U.S. Govt. Print. Off.] 1970. xvi, 456 p.   DS126.5.S6
"DA pam. no. 550–25."

ITALY

359
Italy. *Parlamento.* Annuario parlamentare. 1948/49+ Roma, Segretariato generale della Camera dei deputati.   JN5445.A33

360
Adams, John C., *and* Paolo Barile. The government of republican Italy. 3d ed. Boston, Houghton Mifflin [1972] 248 p.   JN5468.A65 1972
First edition, 1961; second edition, 1966.

361
Annuario d'Italia. Guida generale del regno. [1886–1955?] Genova, G. B. Marsano.
DG413.A6
Volumes for 1892–96 merged with *Calendario generale del Regno d'Italia* (see below). For 1937/38–? a supplemental volume called *Annuario generale d'Italia. Impero Italiano* was published, describing the administration of Libya and Italian East Africa, including Ethiopia (DG413.A62). From 1913, the title was *Annuario generale d'Italia.*

362
Annuario ordinamenti e gerarchie d'Italia; amministrativo, corporativo, sindacale,
    agricolo, industriale, commerciale. [1934–42?] Milano, Casa Editrice Ravagnati.
                                                                    JN5203.A5
        Yearbook of Italian organizations: government, corporate, syndical, agri-
    cultural, industrial, commercial.

363
Annuario politico italiano. [1963–? Milano] Edizioni di comunità.   JN5203.A53

364
Guida ai ministeri ed agli altri uffici pubblici di Roma. [1925–?] Milano.
                                                                    JN5204.G8

365
Guida Monaci; annuario generale di Roma e provincia. [1871]+ Roma.
                                                                    DG804.G8

366
Italy. *Ministero dell' interno.*   Calendario generale del Regno d'Italia. [v. 1–59/60;
    1862–1921/22] Roma.   JN5204
        Volumes for 1892–96 published as part of *Annuario d'Italia* (see above).
    From 1824 to 1860? (v. 1–37?), called *Calendario generale del regno [di
    Sardegna]* (JN5204).

367
Patria nostra; annuario nazionale politico, economico, sociale. [1953/54-?] Roma.
                                                                    DG576.P33

IVORY COAST

368
Annuaire national de la Côte d'Ivoire. [1964+ Douala, Cameroun, Édition "Les
    quatre points cardinaux"]   JQ3386.A423

369
La Côte d'Ivoire administrative. [Abidjan, Eburnea, 1972] 63 p.   JQ3386.A425

370
Mourgeon, Jacques.   La République de Côte d'Ivoire. Paris, Berger-Levrault, 1969.
    47 p. (Encyclopédie politique et constitutionnelle. Série Afrique)
                                                                    JQ3386.A3 1969

371
Roberts, Thomas D., *and others.*   Area handbook for Ivory Coast. 2d ed. [Washing-
    ton, U.S. Govt. Print. Off.] 1973. lxvi, 449 p.   DT545.R58 1973
    "DA pam. no. 550–69."

JAMAICA

372
Handbook of Jamaica . . . comprising historical, statistical and general information
    concerning the island; comp. from official and other reliable records. [1882]+
    Jamaica, Govt. Print. Off.   F1861.H23
                                                                    JL630.A4

373
Gt. Brit. *Colonial Office.* Report on Jamaica. 1946–[61?] London, H.M. Stationery
Off. (*Its* Colonial annual reports) F1861.G7

JAPAN

374
Gyōsei kikan soshiki zu. [Tokyo] Jinjiin. Kanrikyoku. Shokkaika. annual. (Shokkai
kankei shiryō) JQ1601.A27 Orien Japan
Charts of administrative structure of Japanese government.

375
Gyōsei kikō zu. [Tokyo] Gyōsei Kanrichō. Gyōsei Kanrikyoku.
JQ1601.A26 Orien Japan
Charts of Japan's central government organization. Jurisdiction of each
agency explained in separate chapters.

376
Nihon gyōsei kikō yōran. 1+ 1948+ [Tokyo, Gyōsei Kanrichō]
JQ1602.A3 Orien Japan
Handbook of administrative structure of Japan.

377
Shokuinroku. [1886]+ Tokyo, Okurasho. Insatsukyoku. annual. DLC Orien Japan
Directory of government officials.

378
Chaffee, Frederic H., *and others.* Area handbook for Japan. Washington, U.S.
Govt. Print. Off., 1969. xvi, 628 p. DS806.C48
"DA pam. no. 550–30."

379
Gyōsei kikō hensen zu. [Tokyo] Gyōsei Kanrichō. Gyōsei Kanrikyoku [1963] 46 p.
DLC Orien Japan
Diagrams of changes in administrative organization of the Japanese govern-
ment as of June 1963 and changes that took place between 1926 and 1963.

380
Japan. Organization report of Japanese government. [Tokyo] Ministry of Foreign
Affairs, 1949. 353 p. JQ1631.A5
Also issued for 1950 (386, 30 p.).

381
Japan. *Gyōsei Kanrichō.* Chart of Japan's central government organization, compiled by Administrative Management Agency. [Tokyo] Japanese Politics Economy Research Institute, 1960. 130 p. of fold. diagrs., 299 p. JQ1631.A513

382
——— The national administrative organization in Japan. [Tokyo] Administrative
Management Agency, 1972. 30 p. JQ1642.J34 1972

383
——— Organizational charts of Japanese government, as of August 1, 1965. [Tokyo]
Administrative Management Agency. Prime Minister's Office. DLC Orien Japan

384
_____ Table of organization of the government of Japan, September 1970. [Tokyö] Administrative Management Agency, Prime Minister's Office, 1970. 49 p.
JQ1631.A519
Other editions published previously (1967, 1969; JQ1631.A516)

385
Japan. *Naikaku Kambō.* Naikaku seido shichijū-nen shi. [Tokyo] 1955. 2 v.
Seventy-year history of the Cabinet system of Japan. Vol. 2 is a supplement with the title *Naikaku oyobi Sōrifu narabini kakushōchō kiko ichiran* (Diagrams of changes in the government organization from December 1885 to October 1955).

386
The Japan year book. 1933–[1949/52?] Tokyo, Foreign Affairs Association of Japan.   DS803.J52

387
The Japan year book; complete cyclopaedia of general information and statistics on Japan and Japanese territories. 1st–27th year; 1905–31. Tokyo, Japan Year Book Office.   DS803.J5
United with the *Japan Times Yearbook* and published from 1934 to 1941 as *Japan-Manchoukuo Year Book,* and in 1942 as *Orient Year Book* DS803.O7).

388
McNelly, Theodore. Politics and government in Japan. 2d ed. Boston, Houghton Mifflin [1972] 276 p. (Contemporary government series)   JQ1615 1972.M2
1963 ed. published under title: *Contemporary Government of Japan.*

389
Supreme Commander for the Allied Powers. *Government Section.* Report on the organization of the Japanese government, as of 1 August 1946. [Tokyo, 1946–?]
JQ1621.A54

390
U.S. *Embassy. Japan.* The government organization of Japan, with names of bureau, division and section chiefs as of November 20, 1962. Tokyo, Translation Services Branch, Political Section, American Embassy, 1962. 232 p.
JQ1621.U5 1962
Published in 1959 under the title *Revised Japanese and English Language Listing of the Government Organization of Japan.*

391
U.S. *War Dept. General Staff.* Japanese government officials, 1937–1945. Washington, Military Intelligence Division, War Dept. [1945] 169 p.
JQ1621.A5 1945

392
Ward, Robert E. Japan's political system. Englewood Cliffs, N. J., Prentice-Hall [1967] 126 p. (Comparative Asian governments series)   JQ1615 1967.W3

JORDAN

393
Aruri, Naseer H. Jordan: a study in political development (1921–1965). The Hague, Nijhoff, 1972. 206 p.   DS154.5.A78

394
Gt. Brit. *Colonial Office.* Report by His Majesty's government . . . to the council of the League of Nations on the administration of Palestine and Trans-Jordan. 1920/21–[47?] London, H. M. Stationery Off. J693.P22

395
Luke, *Sir* Harry Ch. J., *and* Edward Keith-Roach. The handbook of Palestine and Trans-Jordan. 3d ed. London, Macmillan and Co., 1934. xvi, 549 p.
DS107.3.L8 1934
First edition, 1922; second edition, 1930.

396
Orlov, Evgeniĭ A. Gosudarstvennyĭ stroĭ Iordanii. Moskva, Gos. izd-vo i͡urid. lit-ry, 1961. 60 p. (Gosudarstvennyĭ stroĭ stran mira) JQ1825.J6O7

397
Systems Research Corporation. Area handbook for the Hashemite Kingdom of Jordan. Coauthors: Howard C. Reese and others. Prepared for the American University Foreign Area Studies. Washington, U.S. Govt. Print. Off., 1969. xvi, 370 p. DS153.S95
"DA pam. no. 550–34."

KENYA

398
Directory of the government of the Republic of Kenya. [Nairobi, Office of the President, 1964?]+ JQ2947.A4D57

399
Gt. Brit. *Colonial Office.* Annual report on the Colony and Protectorate of Kenya. 1946–[62?] London, H. M. Stationery Off. (*Its* Colonial annual reports)
DT434.E2A36

400
Kaplan, Irving, *and others.* Area handbook for Kenya. [Washington] 1967. 707 p.
DT434.E2K34
"DA pam. no. 550–56."

401
Kenya Colony and Protectorate. Staff list. Nairobi, Govt. Printer. [1953–62]
JQ2947.A42

402
Kenya. Staff list. 1965+ Nairobi, Govt. Printer. DLC

KHMER REPUBLIC [before 1970: CAMBODIA]

403
Kuo, Shou-hua. Yüeh, Liao, Chien san kuo t'ung chien. Directory of Viet-nam, Laos and Cambodia. Taipei, Central Cultural Supply Agency [1966] 18, 6, 320 p. DS532.5.K86 Orien China

404
U.S. *Embassy (Cambodia)* Leading personalities in Cambodia. Phnom Penh, 1961. 61 l. JQ934.A35

405
Verin, Vladimir P.   Gosudarstvennyĭ stroĭ Kambodzhi. Moskva, Gos. izd-vo ĭurid.
     lit-ry, 1959. 83 p. (Gosudarstvennyĭ stroĭ stran mira)   JQ933 1959.V4

406
Whitaker, Donald P., *and others*.   Area handbook for the Khmer Republic (Cam-
     bodia). [Washington, U.S. Govt. Print. Off.] 1973. xiv, 389 p.   DS554.3.W46
     "DA pam. no. 550–50."

KOREA

407
Chōsen jijō. [1934–44] Keijo.   DS901.C48 Orien Japan
     Annual report on Korea, published by the Government-General.

408
Chōsen yōran. [1923–33] Keijo.   DS901.C49 Orien Japan
     Yearbook of Korea, published by the Government-General.

409
Korea *(Government-General of Chosen, 1910–1945)*   Annual report on administra-
     tion of Chosen. 1907–[44?] Keijo.   DS901.A4

KOREA, DEMOCRATIC PEOPLE'S REPUBLIC OF

410
Baĭanov, Boris P.   Gosudarstvennyĭ stroĭ Koreiskoĭ Narodno-Demokraticheskoĭ Res-
     publiki. Moskva, Gos. izd-vo ĭurid. lit-ry, 1957. 71 p. (Gosudarstvennyĭ stroĭ
     stran mira)   JQ1729.5.A98C423

411
Cho, M. Y.   Die nordkoreanische Führung; Namenverzeichnis mit Einführung.
     Hamburg, 1967. 47, [5] p. (Mitteilungen des Instituts für Asienkunde Ham-
     burg, Nr. 21)   DS1.I55 Nr. 21

412
Korea handbook. Pyongyang, Foreign Languages Pub. House, 1967. 123 p.
                                                              DS932.K567

413
North Korean party organization, March, 1971 [and] North Korean government
     organization, March, 1971. [n. p. 1971]   JQ1729.5.A58N67
     Organization charts, including names of officials.

414
Rudolph, Philip.   North Korea's political and economic structure. New York, Inter-
     national Secretariat, Institute of Pacific Relations, 1959. 72 p.   DS932.R8

415
Shinn, Rinn-Sup, *and others*.   Area handbook for North Korea. Washington, U.S.
     Govt. Print. Off., 1969. xvi, 481 p.   DS932.S5
     "DA pam. no. 550–81."

416
U.S. *Central Intelligence Agency*.   Directory of North Korean officials. [Washington,
     1972] 211 p. (Reference aid)   JQ1729.5.A4U55

417
U.S. *Dept. of the Army.* Communist North Korea; a bibliographic survey. Washington, U.S. Govt. Print. Off., 1971. 130 p.
"DA pam. no. 550–11."
Includes charts of government and military organizations in appendixes.

418
Yang, Key Paik. The North Korean regime, 1945–1955. Washington, 1958, 230 l.
DS935.Y3
Typescript (carbon copy).

KOREA, REPUBLIC OF

419
Chungang yŏn 'gam. 1968+ Seoul, Chungang Ilbasa.   DS901.C52 Orien Korea
Central yearbook [of Korea].

420
Korea annual. 1964+ Seoul, Hapdong News Agency.   DS901.K67

421
Korea directory. 1968+ Seoul [Korea Directory Company]   DS901.K68

422
U.S. *Embassy. Korea.* Principal government officials of the Republic of Korea.
Seoul, [1957?]+   JQ1724.U6

423
American University, *Washington, D.C. Foreign Areas Studies Division.* Area handbook for Korea. Prepared for the Dept. of the Army. Washington, U.S. Govt. Print. Off., 1964. 595 p.   DS902.A63
"DA pam. no. 550–41."
Includes North Korea.

424
Clare, Kenneth G., *and others.* Area handbook for the Republic of Korea. Washington, U.S. Govt. Print. Off., 1969. xiv, 492 p.   DS902.C59 1969
Supersedes DA pam. no. 550–41, 1964 edition.

425
Korea *(Republic) Naegak Samuch 'ŏ.* Chojik p' yŏllam, 1962. [Seoul] 5, 1,252 p.
JQ1725.A5 Orien Korea
Government organization directory.

426
Kuo, Shou-hua. Ta Han min kuo t'ung chien. Directory of Korea.
Taipei, Central Cultural Supply Agency [1967] 14, 191 p.
DS902.K84 Orien China

427
Pak, Tong-sŏ. Han'guk kwallyo chedo ŭi yŏksajŏk chŏn'gae. Seoul, Han'guk Yŏn'gu Tosŏgwan, 1961. 243, 17 p. (Korean studies series, v. 11: Public administration)   JQ1726.P3 Orien Korea
The historical development of the bureaucracy in Korea.

428
Sŏul Taehakkyo. *Haengjŏng Taehagwŏn*. Taehan Min'guk Chŏngbu kigu top'yo
mit haesŏl. [Seoul] 1960. 238 p. (Research series, no. 2)   JQ1726.S6
   Organization and functions of the Republic of Korea Government.

429
U.S. *Army, Korea Civil Assistance Command*   Reference handbook, government of
   the Republic of Korea. [n. p.] 1953. 183 p.   JQ1723 1953
   A revision and enlargement of a similar volume published in 1949 by the
   Economic Cooperation Administration, Mission to Korea.

KUWAIT

430
Stanford Research Institute. Area handbook for the Peripheral States of the
   Arabian Peninsula. Prepared for the American University. [Washington, U.S.
   Govt. Print Off.] 1971. xiv, 201 p.   DS247.A14S78
      "DA pam. no. 550-92."
      Kuwait: p. 95-124.

LAOS

431
Halpern, Joel M.   Government, politics, and social structure in Laos; a study of
   tradition and innovation. [New Haven] Southeast Asia Studies, Yale University; [distributed by the Cellar Book Shop, Detroit, 1964] 184, [13] p. (Yale
   University Southeast Asia Studies. Monograph series, no. 4)   HN700.L3H33

432
Kuo, Shou-hua.   Yüeh, Liao, Chien san kuo t'ung chien. Directory of Viet-nam,
   Laos and Cambodia. Taipei, Central Cultural Supply Agency [1966] 18, 6,
   320 p.   DS532.5.K86 Orien China

433
Laos *(Kingdom)* Le Royaume du Laos, ses institutions et son organisation générale.
   [Vientiane?] 1950. 154 p.   JQ951.A11 1950
      In Lao and French.

434
Okonishnikov, Alekseĭ P.   Gosudarstvennyĭ stroĭ Laosa. Moskva, Gos. izd-vo iūrid.
   lit-ry, 1959. 42 p. (Gosudarstvennyĭ stroĭ stran mira)   JQ953 1959.O4

435
Whitaker, Donald P., *and others*.   Area handbook for Laos. [Washington, U.S.
   Govt. Print Off.] 1972. xiv, 337 p.   DS557.L2W5
      "DA pam. no. 550-58."

LEBANON

436
U.S. *Embassy. Lebanon*. Lebanese government officials and religious leaders.
   [1960?]+ Beirut. annual.   JQ1825.L4U5

437
Who's who in Lebanon. 1.+ éd.; 1963–64+ Beyrouth. Éditions Publictec. biennial.
DS80.75.W5
  In French. Lists all previous governments from 1943.

438
Dadiani, Lionel' ÎA. Gosudarstvennyĭ stroĭ Livana. Moskva, ÎUrid. lit., 1973. 87 p.
JQ1825.L4D3

439
Grassmuck, George L., *and* Kamal Salibi. Reformed administration in Lebanon.
 [2d ed. Ann Arbor, Center for Near Eastern and North African Studies, University of Michigan, 1964] 95 p.   JQ1825.L4G68 1964
  First edition published in 1955 under title: *A Manual of Lebanese Administration* (Beirut, Public Administration Dept., American University of
 Beirut).

440
Smith, Harvey H., *and others*. Area handbook for Lebanon. Washington, U.S.
 Govt. Print Off., 1969. xviii, 352 p.   DS80.S63
 "DA pam. no. 550-24."

LESOTHO [before 1966: BASUTOLAND]

441
Lesotho. *Dept. of Information.* Lesotho; report for the year. [1966?]+ Maseru.
DLC
  Includes description of government agencies and their functions.

442
Gt. Brit. *Colonial Office.* Annual report on Basutoland. 1946–[63?] London, H. M.
 Stationery Off. (*Its* Colonial annual reports)   DT781.A35

LIBERIA

443
Directory with Who's Who in Liberia. 1st+ ed.; 1970/71+ Monrovia A. & A.
 Enterprises.   DT623.D57

444
The Liberia annual review. 1966/67+ Monrovia, Providence Publications.
JQ3921.A1L5
  An earlier edition was published for 1960/61 in London and Monrovia
 (JQ3921.A1L49).

445
Liberia. Handbook of Liberia. [New York, Minden Press] 1940. 61, [3] p.
DT624.A5

446
The Liberian year book. 1956–? London, Diplomatic Press and Pub. Co.
DT621.L53

447
Roberts, Thomas D., *and others.* Area handbook for Liberia. [Washington, U.S. Govt. Print. Off.] 1972. xlviii, 387 p.   DT624.R6 1972
"DA pam. no. 550–38."

448
Tixier, Gilbert. La République du Libéria. Paris, Berger-Levrault, 1970. 49 p. (Encyclopédie politique et constitutionnelle. Série Afrique)   JQ3922.T56

449
The Twentieth century calendar & handbook of Liberia for [1940–?] Liverpool, J. A. Thompson.   DT623.T85

LIBYA

450
Khadduri, Majid. Modern Libya: a study in political development. Baltimore, Johns Hopkins Press, 1963. 404 p.   DT236.K5

451
Nyrop, Richard F., *and others.* Area handbook for Libya. 2d. ed. [Washington, U.S. Govt. Print. Off.] 1973. xv, 317 p.   DT215.N97 1973
"DA pam. no. 550–85."

For the colonial period, see:

452
Annuario delle colonie italiane. [1926–40?] Roma, Cooperativa tipografica "Castaldi."   JV2201.A4
Title for 1937: *Annuario dell'impero italiano;* for 1938–40: *Annuario dell'Africa italiana.*

LUXEMBURG [LUXEMBOURG]

453
Luxemburg *(Grand Duchy)* Annuaire officiel.   [1.]+ année; 1910+ Luxembourg.
JN6381.A11
Publication suspended, 1941–45.

454
Carnegie Endowment for International Peace. *Library.* European governments in exile. Compiled by Helen L. Scanlon. [Washington, 1943] 24 p. (*Its* Memoranda series, no. 3. Revised January 25, 1943)   JX1906.A35 no. 3a
Originally published in 1942.
Luxemburg: p. 12.

455
Majerus, Pierre. The institutions of the Grand Duchy of Luxembourg. Luxembourg, Ministry of State, Press and Information Service, 1970. 80 p. (Acquaintance with Luxembourg, no. 2)   JN6383 1970.M33

MALAGASY REPUBLIC [MADAGASCAR]

456
Malagasy Republic. Annuaire national. [1963?+ Paris, Société Les quatre points
cardinaux]   DT469.M21M3

457
Annuaire du monde politique de la République malgache et du monde économique.
1.–? éd.; 1959–? Tananarive, Agence malgache de presse.   JQ3451.A153

458
Cadoux, Charles.   La République malgache. Paris, Berger-Levrault, 1969. 126 p.
(Encyclopédie politique et constitutionnelle. Série Afrique)   JQ3453 1969.C3

459
Madagascar. Annuaire général. [1892–1926? Tananarive, Imp. officielle] JQ3457.A3

460
Nelson, Harold D., *and others.*   Area handbook for the Malagasy Republic. [Wash-
ington, U.S. Govt. Print. Off.] 1973. xiv, 327 p.   DT469.M26N4
"DA pam. no. 550–163."

461
U.S. *Embassy. Malagasy Republic.* Répertoire pratique: personalités, organismes
gouvernementaux et privés à Madagascar. 1962–? Tananarive.   JQ3457.U5

MALAWI   [before 1964: NYASALAND]

462
Malawi. Government directory. [1966?]+ Zomba, Govt. Printer.   JQ2941.A4A32

463
Gt. Brit. *Colonial Office.*   Annual report on Nyasaland. 1946–[62?] London, H. M.
Stationery Off. (*Its* Colonial annual reports)   DT862.A55

464
Nyasaland. A handbook of Nyasaland. Compiled by S. S. Murray. London [Printed
by Waterlow & Sons] 1932. 436, xi–xxxviii p.   DT858.A5

465
Rhodesia and Nyasaland. *Federal Information Dept.*   Federal and territorial government lists. [1958–62?] Salisbury.   JQ2784.A3

466
_____ Handbook to the Federation of Rhodesia and Nyasaland, Edited by W. V.
Brelsford, Director of Information. [London, Cassel, 1960] 803 p. DT856.A47

467
The Rhodesia-Zambia-Malawi directory (including Botswana and Moçambique).
[1910]+ Bulawayo, Publications (Central Africa). annual.   DT947.R5
Title varies.

MALAYSIA

468
Malaysia. Official year book. v. 1+ 1961+ Kuala Lumpur, Govt. Press. annual.
DS591.A27
Volumes for 1961 and 1962 issued by the Federation of Malaya.

469
Malaysia year book. 1st+ 1963/64+ [Kuala Lumpur] Straits Times Press. annual.
DS591.M38
"A Malay Mail publication."
Superseded *Federation of Malaya Year Book* (see below).

470
Federation of Malaya year book [1956?]–62. [Kuala Lumpur] Straits Times Press.
annual.   DS591.F4
"A Malay Mail publication."
Superseded by *Malaysia Year Book* (see above).

471
Gt. Brit. *Colonial Office.* Report on the Malayan Union. [1947–56] London, H. M.
Stationery Off. (*Its* Colonial annual reports)   DS591.G72
Title varies.

472
Handbook to British Malaya. 1926–[37?] London, Malay States Information
Agency.   DS592.H15

473
Henderson, John W., *and others.* Area handbook for Malaysia. [Washington, U.S.
Govt. Print. Off.] 1970. xvi, 639 p.   DS592.H45 1970
"DA pam. no. 550–45."

474
Malay States, Federated. Year book, 1924–[32] Kuala Lumpur, Federated Malay
States Govt. Print. Off. 9 v.   JQ694 .date c

475
Organisation of the Government of Malaysia. [1967–?] Kuala Lumpur, Di-chetak
di-Jabatan Chetak Kerajaan.   JQ711.A11O75

MALI   [before 1958: FRENCH SUDAN]

476
Bamako. Chambre de Commerce. Gouvernement, Assemblée Nationale et représenta-
tions diverses de la République du Mali. [1962–64?] Bamako.   JQ3389.A4B32

477
Bamako. Chambre de commerce, d'agriculture et d'industrie. Annuaire administratif de la République du Mali. [1964/65–?] Bamako.   DLC

MALTA

478
The Malta year book. [1953]+ St. Julian's, St. Michael's College Publications.
DG987.M33

479
The Malta almanack and directory. [1868–84? Valletta] L. Critien.   DG987.M285

480
The Malta directory & trade index. 1956–[1960/61? Valletta] Malta Publicity Services.   DG989.M25

MAURITANIA

481
Curran, Brian D., *and* Joann Schrock.   Area handbook for Mauritania. [Washington, U.S. Govt. Print. Off.] 1972. xiv, 185 p.   DT553.M2C87
   "DA pam. no. 550–161."

482
Gerteiny, Alfred G.   Mauritania. London, Pall Mall Press, 1967. 243 p. (Pall Mall library of African affairs)   DT553.M2G4 1967

483
Piquemal-Pastré, Marcel.   La République islamique de Mauritanie. Paris, Berger-Levrault, 1969. 52 p. (Encyclopédie politique et constitutionnelle, Série Afrique)
JQ3391.A3 1969.P56

MAURITIUS

484
Mauritius. Staff list. [1948?]+ Port Louis, Govt. Printer.   JQ3167.A35
   Title varies 1948–53, *Mauritius General Clerical Service List;* 1954–59,
   Mauritius Executive Grades and General Clerical Service List.

485
Favoreu, Louis.   L'île Maurice. Paris, Berger-Levrault, 1970. 119 p. (Encyclopédie politique et constitutionnelle. Série Afrique)   JQ3162.F36

486
Gt. Brit. *Colonial Office.*   Annual report on Mauritius. 1946–[64] London, H. M. Stationery Off. (*Its* Colonial annual reports)   DT469.M4A14

487
———— Report on Mauritius. 1949–64. Port Louis, Govt. Printer. 16 v.
HC517.M5A18

488
Gt. Brit. *Commonwealth Office.*   Report on Mauritius. 1965–[67] Port Louis, Govt. Printer.   HC517.M5A19

489
The Mauritius almanac. [1864–1939/41?] Port Louis.   DT469.M4M4
     Section B includes the Mauritius civil list.

490
Mauritius quarterly directory. [1942–?] Port Louis.   DT469.M4M43
     Superseded *Mauritius Quarterly Military Directory*, issued 1899–1941.

MEXICO

491
Directorio del poder ejecutivo federal. [1961]+ México, Secretaría del Patrimonio
     Nacional.   JL1221.A24

492
Mexico. *Secretaría de la Presidencia. Comisión de Administración Pública.*   Manual
     de organización del Gobierno Federal 1969–1970. [México]   DLC

493
Mexico. *Dirección Técnica de Organización Administrativa.*   Directorio del Gobierno
     Federal de los Estados Unidos Mexicanos. 1947–[56] México.   JL1221.A23

494
Mexico. *Secretaría del Patrimonio Nacional.*   Directorio general de organismos
     descentralizados, empresas de participación estatal, establecimientos públicos,
     comisiones, juntas e institutos dependientes del Gobierno Federal. México,
     1964. 65 p.   JL1221.A5

495
Ryan, John M., *and others.*   Area handbook for Mexico. [Washington, U.S. Govt.
     Print. Off.] 1970 [i.e. 1974] xvi, 543 p.   F1208.R98
     "DA pam. no. 550–79."

496
Sáenz de Miera Gamboa, Marco A.   El poder ejecutivo. México, 1963 146 p.
                                                           JL1241.S3
     Tesis (licenciatura en derecho)—Universidad Nacional Autónoma de
     México. Part two deals with the historical development of the Mexican
     government.

497
Scott, Robert E.   Mexican government in transition. Rev. ed. Urbana, University
     of Illinois Press, 1964. 345 p. (Illini books, IB–20)   JL1231.S35 1964

MONACO

498
Monaco.   Annuaire officiel de la principauté de Monaco. [1878]+ Monaco.
                                                            JN3137.A2

MONGOLIA

499
Historical Evaluation and Research Organization, *Washington, D.C.* Area hand-
book for Mongolia. Coauthors: Trevor N. Dupuy [and others] Prepared for
the American University. Washington, U.S. Govt. Print. Off., 1970. xiv, 500 p.
DS798.H57
"DA pam. no. 550–76."

500
Mongol'skaĩa Narodnaĩa Respublika. Moskva, "Nauka," 1971. 438 p. DS798.M5765

501
Sanders, Alan J. K. The People's Republic of Mongolia: a general reference guide.
London, New York, Oxford University Press, 1968. 232 p. DS798.S33

502
Titkov, Vasiliĭ I. Gosudarstvennyĭ stroĭ Mongol'skoĭ Narodnoĭ Respubliki. Moskva,
Gos. izd-vo iŭrid. lit-ry, 1961. 90 p. (Gosudarstvennyĭ stroĭ stran mira)
JQ1519.M6T5

MOROCCO

503
Annuaire marocain. [1929–?] Casablanca, Imprimeries réunies. HC591.M8A65

504
Liste non-officielle du gouvernement marocain. [Rabat? 1962?+] JQ3944.L5

505
Morocco. *Wizārat al-Dākhilīyah.* Dalīl al-mutaṣarrif. [Rabat, 1960?] 379 p.
JQ3945.A8 Orien Arab
Government directory.

506
Nyrop, Richard F., *and others.* Area handbook for Morocco. [Washington, U.S.
Govt. Print. Off.] 1972. xiv, 403 p. DT305.A74 1972
"DA pam. no. 550–49."

NAURU

507
Henderson, John W., *and others.* Area handbook for Oceania. [Washington, U.S.
Govt. Print. Off.] 1971. xiv, 555 p. DU17.H45
"DA pam. no. 550–94."
Nauru: p. 200–202.

508
Packett, C. Neville. Guide to the Republic of Nauru. Bradford, C. N. Packett
[1971] 18 p. DU715.P3

509
Viviani, Nancy. Nauru, phosphate and political progress. Canberra, Australian National University Press, 1970. xiv, 215 p. DU715.V55

NEPAL

510
Nepal. *Dept. of Information.* Kendrīya kāryālaya-harūko nirdeṣikā. Kathmandu,
1971. 29 p.   JQ1825.N44A44
       Directory of central government offices.

511
Nepal. *Dept. of Publicity.* Organisation of His Majesty's Government of Nepal.
[Kathmandu, 1964] 28 p.   JQ1825.N4A53

512
U.S. *Embassy (Nepal)* His Majesty's Government of Nepal: organization chart of
the executive, the judiciary and other official bodies and list of zonal and district
personnel. 1967+ Kathmandu.   JQ1825.N42U5

513
Harris, George L., *and others.* Area handbook for Nepal, Bhutan and Sikkim, 2d ed.
[Washington, U.S. Govt. Print. Off.] 1973. lxxx, 431 p.   DS493.4.H37 1973
"DA pam. no. 550–35."

514
Pradhan, Krishna P. Government and administration and local government of the
Kingdom of Nepal. [Kathmandu, Sudarsun P. Pradhan & Kanhaiya P. Pradhan,
1969] 10, 177 p.   JQ1825.N4P67

515
Shresta, Mangal K. A handbook of public administration in Nepal. [Kathmandu]
Dept. of Publicity, Ministry of Panchayat Affairs [1965] 120 [2] p.
                                                              JQ1825.N42S48

NETHERLANDS

516
Netherlands *(Kingdom, 1815–)* Staatsalmanak voor het Koninkrijk der Nederlanden. [1815]+'s Gravenhage.   JN5704
       Title for 1942/43 and 1943/44 (under German occupation): *Bestuursal-
manak voor het bezette nederlandsche gebied.*

517
Netherlands *(Kingdom, 1815–)* Hof-rijks- en residentie-almanak voor het Koninkrijk
der Nederlanden en zijne koloniën. [1825–1903?] 's Gravenhage
                                                              JN5704.A2
       Title varies.

518
Netherlands *(Kingdom, 1815–)* *Departement van Buitenlandse Zaken.* The Kingdom
of the Netherlands. Facts and figures. The Hague, Govt. Print. Off., 1971.
890 p.   DJ18.A45

519
Pyttersen's nederlandse almanak. [1900]+ Zaltbommel, van de Garde. JN5703.N4
       Title varies.

For the government in exile (1940–45), see:

520
Carnegie Endowment for International Peace. *Library.* European governments in exile. Compiled by Helen L. Scanlon. [Washington, 1943.] 24 p. (*Its* Memoranda series, no. 3. Revised January 25, 1943) JX1906.A35 no. 3a
   Originally published in 1942.
   Netherlands: p. 13–14.

521
Netherlands (*Kingdom, 1815–*) *Departement van Buitenlandse Zaken.* The list of the Netherlands government. [London] Ministry for Foreign Affairs, 1943. 16 p.
 JN5704.A5 1943

NEW ZEALAND

522
Cleveland, Les, *and* A. D. Robinson.   Readings in New Zealand government. Wellington, Reed Education, 1972. 314 p. JQ811.C5

523
Polaschek, R. J.   Government administration in New Zealand. Wellington, New Zealand Institute of Public Administration, 1958. 324 p. JQ5831.P6

NICARAGUA

524
Caldera, J. M.   Directorio oficial de Nicaragua. Managua [J. M. Caldera] 1923. 644 p. F1522.3.C14

525
Guía económica de Nicaragua. 1957–? Managua. HC147.N6G8
   "Directorio de organismos del Estado," p. 103–107.

526
Pan American Union.   Nicaragua. 1909–[56?] Washington, D.C. F1523.P2
   Includes a short description of the central government.

527
Ryan, M., *and others.*   Area handbook for Nicaragua. Prepared for the American University by Johnson Research Associates. [Washington, U.S. Govt. Print. Off.] 1970. xvi, 393 p. F1523.R9
   "DA pam. no. 550–88."

NIGER

528
Beuchelt, Eno.   Niger. Bonn, K. Schroeder, 1968. 143 p. (Die Länder Afrikas, Bd. 38) DT547.B4
   In German.

529
Donaint, Pierre, *and* François Lancrenon.   Le Niger. Paris, Presses universitaires de France, 1972. 126 p. (Que sais-je? No. 1461) DT547.2.D65

530
Niger.   Organigramme du gouvernement de la République du Niger; janvier 1964.
    Niamey, 15 l.   DLC

531
République du Niger. [Paris, Larousse, 1964] 31 p.   DT547.R4
        Separately published section from *Encyclopédie africaine et malgache*
    Larousse.

NIGERIA

532
Nigeria. *Ministry of Internal Affairs.*   Office directory, Lagos area. [1958]+ Lagos,
    Federal Ministry of Information, Print. Division. semiannual.   JQ3087.A34

533
Gt. Brit. *Colonial Office.*   Annual report on Nigeria. 1946–[57?] London, H. M.
    Stationery Off. (*Its* Colonial annual reports)   DT515.A573

534
Murray, D. J., J. Barbour, *and* E. O. Kowe.   The progress of Nigerian public admin-
    istration; a report on research. [Ibadan, Institute of Administration, University
    of Ife, Nigeria, 1968] xx, 238 p.   Z7165.N5M9

535
Nelson, Harold D., *and others.*   Area handbook for Nigeria. [Rev. 3d ed. Washington,
    U.S. Govt. Print. Off.] 1972. xvi 485 p.   DT515.N37 1972
    "DA pam. no. 550–157."

536
Nigeria.   The Nigeria handbook. [1953–?] London, Crown Agents for Oversea
    Governments and Administrations.   DT515.A44

537
Nigeria.   Staff list. Lagos.   JQ3087.A33
        Title varies: –1944, *Classified Staff List.*
        Current title: *Federal Staff List.*

538
Nigeria. *Chief Secretary's Office.*   The Nigeria civil service list. [1928–?] Lagos.
                                                                       JQ3087.A3

539
_____ The Nigeria handbook containing statistical and general information respect-
    ing the colony and protectorate. [1917–36?] Lagos, Govt. Printer. DT515.A45

540
Nigeria handbook, 1970. [Lagos, Federal Ministry of Information, 1971?] 221 p.
                                                                       DT515.N46

541
Nigeria yearbook. [1952+ Lagos, Nigerian Print. and Pub. Co.]   DT515.N48
    "A Daily Times publication."

542

Pacific Printers, *Yaba, Nigeria.*   The independent Nigeria, October 1, 1960. Yaba
[1960] 159 p.   DT515.P18

543

Wey, S. O.   The structure and organisation of the public services. [Lagos] 1971.
63 l.   JQ3092.W48

NORWAY

544

Norway.   Norges statskalender. 1815+   Oslo.   JN7405
Title varies.
Irregular, 1815–75; annual, 1877+

545

Carnegie Endowment for International Peace. *Library.*   European governments in
exile. Compiled by Helen L. Scanlon. [Washington, 1943] 24 p. (*Its* Memoranda series, no. 3. Revised January 25, 1943)   JX1906.A35 no. 3a
Originally published in 1942.
Norway: p. 15–16.

546

Duffy, Frank J.   The political institutions and government of Norway; a survey.
Oslo, University of Oslo, 1953. 120 l.   JN7445 1953.D8

547

Lehmkuhl, Dik.   Journey to London; the story of the Norwegian government at
war. London, New York, Hutchinson & Co. [1946] 152 p.   D763.N6L39

548

Mannheimer, Kaj.   Norge och den norska exilregeringen under andra världskriget.
Stockholm, Allmannaförlaget, (Justitiedepartementet) 1972. 165 p. (Statens
offentliga utredningar, 1972: 18)   J406.R15 1972:18
Norway and Norwegian exile governments during World War II.

549

Nasjonal samling. NS årbok. [1942, Oslo] Blix, 1942. 208 p.   JN7691.N3
Yearbook of the National Assembly. Includes list of government agencies
under German occupation. Issued by Rikspropagandaledelsen.

550

Norway. *Statsministeren.*   Statsminister Johan Nygaardsvolds beretning om Den
norske regjerings virksamhet fra 9 april 1940 til 25 juni 1945. Utg. av Stortin-
get. Oslo, H. Aschehong, 1947. 45 p.   D763.N6A5 1947
A report of State Minister Johan Nygaardsvolds on the activities of the
Norwegian government from April 9, 1940, to June 25, 1945.

PAKISTAN

551

Pakistan. *Cabinet Secretariat.*   The official and diplomatic directory. [1954?]+
Karachi, Manager, Govt. of Pakistan Press.   JQ547.A32

552
Pakistan. *Establishment Division.* Civil list of class I officers serving under government of Pakistan. Jan. 1961+ Karachi, Manager of Publications.   JQ547.A34

553
Nyrop, Richard F., *and others.* Area handbook for Pakistan. [Washington, U.S. Govt. Print Off.] 1971. xvi, 691 p.   DS377.N97
    "DA pam. no. 550–48."

554
Pakistan. *Cabinet Division.* The official directory; a list of central and provincial officers of and above the status of deputy secretary to the Central Government. Rawalpindi [1966] 44 p.   JQ547.A5

555
Pakistan. *Cabinet Secretariat.* Administrative directory of the government of Pakistan. [1949–51, Karachi]   JQ547.P28

556
The Pakistan civil list; a complete directory of the Pakistan civil service and other higher services under Government. no. 1–? Oct./Dec. 1950–? [Lahore]
    JQ547.P3

557
Pakistan year-book. 1969+ [Karachi, National Pub. House]   DS376.P3488
    Continues the monograph: *Twenty Years of Pakistan, 1947–67* (Karachi, Pakistan Publications, 1967. DS384.T9).

558
The Pakistan year book & who's who. 1st–? 1949–? Karachi, Kitabistan. DS376.P35

559
Williams, Laurence F. R. The State of Pakistan. Rev. ed. London, Faber, 1966.
    262 p.   DS384.W54 1966

PANAMA

560
Guía general de la República de Panamá (aprobada por el gobierno). Panamá, Impr. Nacional, 1932. 311 p.   F1563.G92

561
Panama. *Departamento de Organización Administrativa.* Diagnóstico de la administración pública y planteamientos para su fortalecimiento. [Panamá, 1970] 213 p.   JL1650.A5

562
—— Manual de organización del Gobierno de Panamá. Panamá, 1961. 202 p.
    JL1650.A53

563
Panama (City) Biblioteca Nacional. Guía de organismos oficiales y sus publicaciones. Panamá, 1960. 29 p.

564
Weil, Thomas E., *and others*. Area handbook for Panama. [Washington, U.S. Govt. Print. Off.] 1972. 415 p. F1563.W36 "DA pam. no. 550–46."

PARAGUAY

565
Asunción. Universidad nacional. *Escuela Paraguaya de Administración Pública.* Manual del gobierno paraguayo. [2. ed. Asunción] 1965. 90 p. JL3231.A85 1965

566
Guía general de la República del Paraguay; noticia general de su comercio, industria, agricultura, etc. Datos de su gobierno, administración, leyes. [1893–1920?] Asunción. F2664.5.G93

567
Guía general del Paraguay; anuario. [1906–?] Asunción. F2664.5.G94

568
Paraguay. *Dirección General de Presupuesto.* Anexo del personal de la administración central, ejercicio fiscal, 1971. Asunción, Impr. Nacional [1971] 263 p. JL3249.S2A45

569
Ricca, Serafín J. Los Ministerios para el desarrollo: sus funciones y competencias. Asunción, Division de Administración para el Desarrollo, Secretaría Técnica de Planificación del Desarrollo Económico y Social, 1968. 102 p. JL3242.R53

570
Weil, Thomas E., *and others*. Area handbook for Paraguay. [Washington, U.S. Govt. Print. Off.] 1972. xiv, 316 p. F2668.W4 "DA pam. no. 550–156."

PERU

571
Peru. *Oficina Nacional de Racionalización y Capacitación de la Administración Pública.* Directorio del gobierno peruano. [2. ed. Lima, 1967] 496 p. JL3421.A3 1967

572
—— Guía del gobierno peruano. [Lima] 1966. 294 p. JL3426 1966.A5

573
American University, *Washington, D. C. Foreign Areas Studies Division.* Area handbook for Peru. Coauthors: Thomas E. Weil [and others. Washington, U.S. Govt. Print. Off.] 1972. 429 p. F3408.A75 1972 "DA pam. no. 550–42."

574
Anuario nacional peruano; gran revista administrativa, legislativa, judicial, comercial. [1930–?] Lima, A. Belaúnde. F3401.A53

575
Calendario [del Peru, 1859-?] Lima.   JL3421.C3

576
Calendario y guía de forasteros de la República Peruana. [1800-?] Lima. JL3402.C3
    Title varies.

577
Directorio anual del Perú. 1-? año; 1910-? Lima, Impr. del Estado.   F3404.5.D59

578
Directorio general del Perú; guía completa de la República, comprendiendo todas
    sus provincias. Lima, 1914. 124, 760 p.   F3404.5.D6

579
Guía política, eclesiástica y militar del Vireynato del Perú. 1793-97. [Lima] Impresa
    en la Impr. Real de los Niños Huérfanos. 5 v.   JL3400.A4A3 Rare Book Coll.

PHILIPPINES

580
Philippines (*Republic*) *Office of Public Information.* Official directory of the Repub-
    lic of the Philippines. [1946]+ Manila, Bureau of Printing.   JQ1407.A3

581
Abueva, Jose V., *and* Raul P. de Guzman.   Handbook of Philippine public adminis-
    tration. [Manila, Social Research Associates, 1967] 523 p.   JQ1410.A57

582
Andaya, Araceli.   An annotated bibliography on Philippine public administration.
    Manila, Institute of Public Administration, University of the Philippines, 1953.
    53 l.   Z7165.P5A8

583
Chaffee, Frederic E., *and others.*   Area handbook for the Philippines. Washington,
    U.S. Govt. Print. Off., 1969. xiv, 413 p.   DS655.C4
    "DA pam. no. 550-72."

584
Chicago. University. *Philippine Studies Program.*   Area handbook on the Philippines.
    Prelim. ed. [Chicago] University of Chicago for the Human Relations Area
    Files, 1956. 4 v. (xxxiv, 1832 p.)   DS655.C45

585
Jacobini, H. B. *ed.*   Governmental services in the Philippines. Manila, Institute of
    Public Administration, University of the Philippines, 1956. 640 p. (University
    of the Philippines. Institute of Public Administration. Studies in public admin-
    istration, no. 3)   JQ1410.J3

586
Philippine Islands.   Guía oficial de las islas Filipinas. [1834?-98] Manila.
                                                                      JQ1251.A11

587

―――― Handbook on the executive departments of the government of the Philippine Islands. Manila, Bureau of Print., 1912. 5–172 p.   JQ1340.A5 1912

588

Philippine Islands. *Bureau of Civil Service.* Official roster of officers and employees in the civil service of the Philippine Islands. 1902–? Manila, Bureau of Print.
                                                                                JQ1321

589

Philippines *(Republic) Institute of National Language.* Mga katawagáng pampá-mahalaán. Government terms. Bagong edisyon. Manila, Bureau of Print., 1956. 53 p. (Publications of the Institute of National Language)   JQ1410.A5 1956
     An earlier edition was issued in 1951. Contains list of names of government agencies and subdivisions in English and Tagalog.

590

Philippines *(Republic) Office of Public Information.* Republic of the Philippines government manual. 1st–? ed.; 1950–? Manila, Bureau of Print.   JQ1401.A12

591

U.S. *Office of Strategic Services. Research and Analysis Branch.* The government of the "New Philippines": a study of the present puppet government in the Philippines. [Washington] 1944. 54 p. (*Its* Report no. 1752)
                                                                UB250.U33 no. 1752

―――― Status of the Philippine puppet government as of 14 October 1944, a supplement. [Washington] 1944. 17 p. (*Its* R & A no. 1752.2)
                                                                UB250.U33 no. 1752.2

592

―――― Personnel of the Philippine puppet government. [Washington] 1944. 29 l. (*Its* R & A no. 1752.1)   UB250.U33 no. 1752.1

POLAND

593

Rocznik polityczny i gospodarczy. 1932+ [Warszawa] Państwowe Wydawn. Ekono-miczne.   JN6751.A17
     Suspended 1940–47, 1949–57.
     Political and economic yearbook.

_____

594

Directory of Polish officials. [1973]+ [Washington] Central Intelligence Agency.
     (Reference aid)   JN6757.D55

595

Directory of Polish officials. [n. p.] 1970. 346 p.   JN6757 1970.D56

596

Directory of Polish officials; intelligence research aid. [n. p.] 1966. 233 p.
                                                                JN6757 1966.D5

597
Gwiżdż, Andrzej. Gosudarstvennyĭ stroĭ Polskoĭ Narodnoĭ Respubliki. [Perevod s
pol'skogo Iriny Dudovskoĭ] Varshava, Poloniîa, 1966. 85 p.　　JN6753 1966.G9

598
Keefe, Eugene K., and others. Area handbook for Poland. [Washington, U.S. Govt.
Print. Off.] 1973. xiv, 335 p.　　　　　　　　　　　　　　DK443.K38
"DA pam. no. 550–162."

599
Morrison, James F. The Polish People's Republic. Baltimore, Johns Hopkins Press
[1968] xx, 160 p. (Integration and community building in Eastern Europe,
JH-EE 2)　　　　　　　　　　　　　　　　　　　　　　　DK443.M65

600
Poland. Ministerstwo Komunikacji. Wydzial Turystyki Ogólnej i Akwizycji. Infor-
mator o urzędach, instytucjach publicznych, środkach komunikacji, uzdrowis-
kach i hotelach v Polsce. [1946–?] Warszawa.　　　　　　　DK403.A33
Directory of offices, public institutions, communications, etc.

601
Polish regime directory, November 1957. [Warsaw? 1957] 103 l.　　JN6757.P63

602
Sobolewski, Marek, comp. Ustrój Polski Ludowej na tle porownawczym. Kraków,
1965. 226 p.　　　　　　　　　　　　　　　　　　　　　　JN6760.S6
Issued by Uniwersytet Jagieloński. A comparative study of Polish governmental structure.

603
Spis urzędów i instytucyj państwowych Rzeczypospolitej Polskiej. [Warszawa] Nakl.
Polskiej Agencji Telegraficznej, 1936. 224 p.　　　　　　JN6757 1936.S6
List of government agencies and institutions of the Republic of Poland.

604
U.S. Dept. of State. Division of Biographic Information. Directory of Polish officials; personnel in the political parties, government, and mass organizations of
the Polish People's Republic. [Washington] 1960. xxii, 623 p. (Its Biographic
directory, no. 274)　　　　　　　　　　　　　　　　　　DR5.U55 no. 274

For the Polish government in exile (1939–45) and the German administration in occupied Poland, see:

605
Carnegie Endowment for International Peace. Library. European governments in
exile. Compiled by Helen L. Scanlon. [Washington, 1943] 24 p. (Its Memo-
randa series, no. 3. Revised January 25, 1943)　　　　　JX1906.A35 no. 3a
Originally published in 1942.
Poland: p. 17–19.

606
Gingerich, William F. The German administration of the general government of
Poland, 1939–1941. Washington, 1949. 347 l.　　　　　　JN6752.G5
Thesis—Georgetown University.

PORTUGAL

607
Anuário comercial de Portugal. [1880?]+ Lisboa, Emprese Nacional de Publici-
dade.   DP513.A5
Each edition includes a government directory. Title varies: –1893, *Alma-
naque commercial de Lisboa.*

608
Portugal. *Presidência de Conselho.* 25 [i.e. Vinte e cinco] anos de administração
pública. Lisboa, Impr. Nacional, 1953+   JN8536.J65
Contents:—[1] Ministério das Comunicações.—[2] Ministério de Exér-
cito.—[3] Ministério das Finanças.—[4] Ministério do Interior.—[5]
Ministério das Obras Públicas.—[6] Presidência do Conselho.—[7] Ministério do Ultramar.

QATAR

609
Stanford Research Institute. Area handbook for the Peripheral States of the Arabian
Peninsula. Prepared for the American University. [Washington, U.S. Govt.
Print. Off.] 1971. xiv, 201 p.   DS247.A14S78
"DA pam. no. 550–92."
The Gulf States: p. 125–152.

RHODESIA

610
Rhodesia. *Dept. of Information.* Government list. [1967]+ Salisbury. annual. DLC
Before 1967 issued by the Information Service (*Rhodesia Government
List*).

611
Rhodesia, Southern. Official year book of the colony of Southern Rhodesia. [v. 1–4;
1924–52] Salisbury.   DT962.A3
Four volumes, published in 1924, 1930, 1932, and 1952.

612
Rhodesia and Nyasaland. *Federal Information Dept.* Federal and territorial government lists. [1958–62?] Salisbury.   JQ2784.A3

613
The Rhodesia-Zambia-Malawi directory (including Botswana and Moçambique).
[1910]+ Bulawayo, Publications (Central Africa). annual.   DT947.R5
Title varies.

ROMANIA

614
Administrația de stat in Republica Socialistă România [de] Dumitru Holt [et al.]
București, Editura Academiei Republicii Socialiste România, 1968. 360 p.
JN9623 1968.A65

615
Ceterchi, Ioan.   The state system of the Socialist Republic of Romania. Bucarest,
    Meridiane Pub. House, 1967. 130 p.   JN9623 1967.C4713

616
Directory of Rumanian officials. [1964?+ Washington?]   JN9627.D55

617
Keefe, Eugene K., *and others*. Area handbook for Romania. [Washington, U.S.
    Govt. Print. Off.] 1972. xiv, 319 p.   DR205.K43
    "DA pam. no. 550-160."

618
Mitskevich, Aleksei V. Gosudarstvennyĭ stroĭ Rumynskoĭ Narodnoĭ Respubliki.
    Moskva, Gos. izd-vo ĭurid. lit-ry, 1957. 89 p. (Gosudarstvennyĭ stroĭ stran mira)
                                                              JN9623 1945.M5

RWANDA

619
Lemarchand, René. Rwanda and Burundi. New York, Praeger [1970] 562 p.
    (Praeger library of African affairs)   DT449.R442L44 1970

620
Nyrop, Richard F., *and others*. Area handbook for Rwanda. Washington, U.S.
    Govt. Print. Off., 1969. xiv, 212 p.   DT449.R9N9
    "DA pam. no. 550-84."

621
Vanderlinden, Jacques. La République rwandaise. Paris, Berger-Levrault, 1970.
    64 p. (Encyclopédie politique et constitutionnelle. Série Afrique) JQ3567.A2V35

SAUDI ARABIA

622
Arabian American Oil Company. Aramco handbook; oil and the Middle East
    [Rev. ed.] Dhahran [1968] 279 p.   HD9576.A64A72 1968
        First published in 1950 under title: *American Employees Handbook Series*.
        Includes list of government agencies.

623
——— Saudi Arabia: directory of the royal family, officials of the government,
    diplomats and other prominent persons. [4th ed.] Dhahran, 1962+ 1 v.
    (looseleaf)   JQ1825.S32A7

624
Walpole, Norman C., *and others*.   Area handbook for Saudi Arabia. [Washington,
    U.S. Govt. Print. Off.] 1971. xlviii, 373 p.   DS204.W34 1971
    "DA pam. no. 550-51."

SENEGAL

625
American University, *Washington, D.C. Foreign Areas Studies Division.* Area
handbook for Senegal. [Washington, U.S. Govt. Print. Off.] 1963. xiv, 489 p.
DT549.A58
"DA pam. no. 550–70."
A new edition, compiled by Harold D. Nelson, issued in 1974 (DT549.N4).

626
Annuaire du Sénégal et dépendences. [1854–1902] Saint-Louis, Impr. du gouvernement. DT549.A7
Continued by *Annuaire du gouvernement général de l'Afrique occidentale
française* (see below).

627
Directory [of the] Republic of Senegal. [1972]+ Dakar, American Embassy.
JQ3396.A4D56

628
French West Africa. Annuaire du gouvernement général de l'Afrique occidentale
française. [1903–22] Paris. JQ3357.A3

629
Gautron, Jean C. L'administration sénégalaise. Paris, Berger-Levrault, 1971. 95 p.
(Encyclopédie administrative) JQ3396.A55 1971

630
Gonidec, P. F. La République du Sénégal. Paris, Berger-Levrault, 1968. 64 p.
(Encyclopédie politique et constitutionnelle. Série Afrique) JQ3396.A3G6 1968

SIERRA LEONE

631
Sierra Leone year book. [1956]+ Freetown, Daily Mail. DT516.A2S5

632
Gt. Brit. *Colonial Office.* Annual report on Sierra Leone. 1946–[58?] London,
H. M. Stationery Off. (*Its* Colonial annual reports) DT516.A15

633
Sierra Leone. The protectorate handbook. [1955–? Bo.] DT516.A3A34

634
———— Review of government departments. [1960–?] Freetown, Govt. Printer.
J747.R16

SINGAPORE

635
Singapore. Directory [of] Istana Negara, judicial, cabinet, Legislative Assembly,
Public Service Commission, audit, ministries, Industrial Arbitration Court, statutory boards, advisory committees, universities, polytechnic, Commonwealth rep-
resentatives and foreign consuls. [1945?]+ Singapore. JQ745.S5A35

636
_____ Singapore senior establishment staff list. [Singapore, Govt. Print. Off.,
1969+] (looseleaf)   JQ745.S54A5

637
Singapore year book. [1964?]+ Singapore, Govt. Print. Off.   DS598.S7S6
Title varies: 1969+, *Singapore.*

638
Maday, Bela S., *and others.* Area handbook for Malaysia and Singapore. Washing-
ton, U.S. Govt. Print. Off., 1965 [i.e. 1966] 745 p.   DS592.M16
"DA pam. no. 550–45."

639
Singapore. *Colonial Secretary's Office.* Establishment manual. [1953–?] Singapore.
Govt. Print. Off.   JQ745.S5A33

640
The Singapore and Straits directory. [1879–1941?] Singapore.   DS502.S6

641
Srinivasagam, Elizabeth. Guide to Singapore government departments and serials
as of 30th August, 1963. Majallah perpustakaan Singapura. Singapore library
journal. v. 3, April 1964: 70–90.   Z671.M32 v. 3.

SOMALIA

642
Somali Institute of Public Administration. A directory of senior government officials.
[1965]+ Mogadiscio.   JQ3585.A4S6

643
_____ List and functions of public agencies in Somalia. Mogadiscio, 1972. 20 p.
JQ3585.A63S66

644
Annuario delle colonie italiane (e dei paesi vicini). [1926–40?] Roma, Cooperativa
tipografica "Castaldi."   JV2201.A4
Title varies: 1937, *Annuario dell'impero italiano;* 1938–40, *Annuario
dell'Africa italiana.*

645
Gt. Brit. *Colonial Office.* Report on the Somaliland Protectorate. [1948–58/59?]
London, H. M. Stationery Off. (*Its* Colonial annual reports)   DT406.A14

646
Kaplan, Irving, *and others.* Area handbook for Somalia. [Washington, U.S. Govt.
Print. Off.] 1969 [i.e. 1970] xiv, 455 p.   DT401.K33
"DA pam. no. 550–86."

647
Somalia. *Council of Ministers.* Government activities from independence until to-
day. July 1, 1960–December 31, 1963. Mogadiscio, Presidency of the Council of
Ministers, [1964] 199 p.   JQ3585.A5

SOUTH AFRICA

648
Guide to state departments and certain statutory bodies. [1967]+ Johannesburg,
H. McCarthy Publications. annual? JQ1902.G83

649
Kaplan, Irving, *and others.* Area handbook for the Republic of South Africa.
[Washington, U.S. Govt. Print. Off.] 1971. xvi, 845 p. DT753.K3
"DA pam. no. 550-93."

650
South Africa. Public service list. [1914–?] Pretoria. JQ1921.A3

651
South Africa. *Office of Census and Statistics.* Official year book of the Union.
[1–30; 1918–60] Pretoria. DT752.A3
Superseded in part by the Bureau of Statistics' *Statistical Yearbook*
(1964–67. HA1991.A23) and, from 1968, its *Suid-Afrikaanse Statistieke*
(HA1991.A232).
Includes information on the government organization of the Union, Basutoland, Bechuanaland, and Swaziland, from 1910.
An entirely new yearbook, called *South Africa 1974; Official Yearbook of
the Republic of South Africa,* was published in 1974. It includes several chapters on government organization.

SPAIN

652
Spain. *Laws, statutes, etc.* Organización de la administración del Estado. Madrid,
Presidencia del Gobierno, Secretaría General Técnica, 1972. 652 p. DLC LL

653
Spain. *Presidencia del Gobierno.* Guía de la administración del Estado. 1960+
Madrid. JN8104.A32

654
Anuario general de España. 2. epoca, año 1+ 1912+ Barcelona DP11.A7
Formed by the union of the *Anuario del comercio, de la industria, de la
magistratura* . . . and the *Anuario Riera general y exclusiva de España.* Includes in each edition a detailed section on the central government.

655
F. A. C. Ficheros de altos cargos. Madrid, 194?+ DLC
A card directory of the Spanish government, arranged alphabetically by
ministries. Established by Angel Estirado Pérez. An *Indice alfabético* also
issued.

656
García de Enterria, Eduardo. La administración española. Estudios de ciencia administrativa. Madrid, Alianza Editorial [1972] 165 p. (El libro de bolsillo. Sección: Humanidades, v. 389) JN8221.G3 1972

657
Heráldica; guía de sociedad. [1951?]+ Madrid. annual.   DP11.H4
   A substantial section is devoted to the central government.

658
Spain. Guía oficial de España. [1722–1930] Madrid.   JN8104
   Original title: *Kalendario manual y guía de forasteros.*

659
Spain. *Junta Interministerial Commemoradora del xxv Aniversario de la Paz Españ-
   ola.* El Gobierno informa. [Madrid] 1964. 4 v.   DP270.A54
   Contents:—1. Politica de paz: La Jefatura del Estado. La Presidencia del
   Gobierno. El Movimiento Nacional. Los Asuntos Exteriores. La Gobernación
   del Pais.—2. Sociedad española: La Justicia. La Educación Nacional. El Tra-
   bajo. La Información y Turismo. La Vivienda.—3. Defensa Nacional: El
   Ejército. Las fuerzas navales. La aviación.—4. Nueva economía: La Hacienda.
   Las Obras Públicas. La industria. La Agricultura. El Comercio.

660
Spain. *Presidencia del Gobierno. Oficina de Información.* Guía de la administración
   civil del Estado. Madrid. 1963. 375 p.   JN8104.A52

661
Spain. *Presidencia del Gobierno. Secretaría General Técnica.* The organization of
   the Spanish public administration. Madrid [Documentation and Publications of
   the General Technical Secretariat of the Prime Minister's Dept.] 1957. 25 p.
   (*Its* Publications)   DLC LL

SRI LANKA   [before 1972: CEYLON]

662
The Ceylon year book. The official statistical annual of the social, economic and gen-
   eral conditions of the island. 1948+ [Colombo]   DS488.C43
   Includes a section on government organization.

663
Ferguson's Ceylon directory. 1920/21+ Colombo, Associated Newspapers of Ceylon.
   annual.   DS488.9.C4
   Continues *The Ceylon Handbook & Directory and Compendium of Useful
   Information* (published since 1858?).

664
Ceylon.   Ceylon civil list. [1950?+ Colombo] Govt. Press.   JQ654.A35

665
Ceylon. *Colonial Secretary's Office.* The Ceylon civil list. [1866?–1949] Colombo.
          JQ654.A3

666
Gupta, Madan G.   The government of Ceylon, Allahabad, Central Book Depot
   [1965] 45 p.   JQ653 1965.G8

667
Namasivayam, Sagarajasingham.   Parliamentary government in Ceylon, 1948–1958.
   Colombo, K. V. G. De Silva [1959] 125 p.   JQ652.N36

668
Nyrop, Richard F., *and others.* Area handbook for Ceylon. [Washington, U.S. Govt.
Print. Off.] 1971. xvi, 525 p.   DS489.N9
"DA pam. no. 550–96."

SUDAN

669
Sudan. *Wizārat al- I'lām wa-al-Thaqāfah.* Taqwīm al-Sūdān. [1970/71]+ Khar-
toum. annual.   DT118.A37 Orien Arab
Sudan yearbook.

670
Sudan almanac. Official handbook. Compiled by the Ministry of Information. Khartoum, Govt. Print. Press [1903]+   JQ3802

671
U.S. *Embassy (Sudan). Economic Section.* Key officials handbook. [1972]+
Khartoum.   JQ3981.S82U55a

672
Nelson, Harold D., *and others.* Area handbook for the Democratic Republic of
Sudan. [Washington, U.S. Govt. Print. Off.] 1973. xiv, 351 p.   DT121.N44
"DA pam. no. 550–27."

673
Sudan.   Government list. Khartoum [1937–63?]   JQ3981.S8S8
Title and frequency vary.
The 1963 edition called *The Republic of the Sudan Staff List.*

674
Sudan. *Governor-General.* Report on the administration of the Sudan. 1921–
[50?] London, H. M. Stationery Off.   J868.N16

675
The Sudan directory. July 1921–[51/52?] Khartoum, Sudan Advertising & Pub.
Co.   DT118.S8

SWAZILAND

676
Gt. Brit. *Colonial Office.* Swaziland; report. 1946–[66?] London, H. M. Stationery
Off.   HC517.S^A35

677
Swaziland. *Government Information Services.* A handbook to the Kingdom of Swaziland. [Mbabane, 1968] 126 p.   DT971.A44

678
Van Wyk, Adam J. Swaziland; a political study. Pretoria, Africa Institute, 1969.
75 p. (Communications of the Africa Institute, no. 9)   DT1.A143 no. 9

SWEDEN

679
Sweden.   Sveriges statskalender. Utg. efter Kungl. Maj:ts nådigste förordnande af
dess Vetenskapsakademi. 1877+ Uppsala & Stockholm.   JN7724

680
Andrén, Nils B. E.   Modern Swedish government. 2., revid. ed. Stockholm, Almquist
& Wiksell, 1968. 282 p.   JN7825.A7 1968

681
Sweden.   Sveriges och norges stats-kalender. [1764–1876] Stockholm.   JN7724.A32
Title varies.
Superseded in 1877 by *Sveriges statskalender.*

SWITZERLAND

682
Jahrbuch der eidgenössischen Behörden.   Annuaire des autorités fédérales. Annuario
delle autorità federali. 1916+ Bern, Verbandsdruckerei.   JN8703.J3

683
Switzerland.   Staats-kalender der Schweizerischen Eidgenossenschaft. Annuaire de la
Confédération suisse. 1849+ Bern.   JN8704

684
Berner Adressbuch. [1882?]+ Bern, Hallwag. annual.   DQ409.2.A4

685
Politisches Jahrbuch der Schweizerischen Eidgenossenschaft. 1.–31. Jahrg.; 1886–
1917. Bern, K. J. Wyss. 31 v.   DQ1.P7

686
Schweizer Jahrbuch des öffentlichen Lebens.   Annuaire suisse de la vie publique.
1958+ Basel, B. Schwabe.   AY1022.S38
Includes section on the Principality of Liechtenstein.

SYRIA

687
Syria. Directory of Syria. [1966–? Damascus]   DLC
Mimeographed, looseleaf.

688
Hourani, Albert H.   Syria and Lebanon; a political essay. Beirut, Lebanon Bookshop
[1968] 402 p.   DS98.H65 1968
Reprint of the 1946 edition published by Oxford University Press.

689

L'Indicateur syrien commercial, administratif, industriel. 1. année; 1922. Beyrouth, Imprimerie Gédéon, 1922. 320, iv, [226] p.　　　　　　　HF3861.S8I6
　　　At head of title: *Annuaire de la Syrie et du Liban.* In French and Arabic.

690

Nyrop, Richard F., *and others.*　Area handbook for Syria. [Washington, U.S. Govt. Print. Off.] 1971. xiv, 357 p.　　　　　　　　　　　DS93.N9 1971
　　　"DA pam. no. 550–47."
　　　Earlier editions published in 1958 and 1965.

TANZANIA [before 1964: TANGANYIKA and ZANZIBAR]

691

Tanzania.　Directory. [1966?]+ Dar es Salaam.　　　　　　　　JQ3514.A23
　　　Earlier editions called *Tanganyika Directory.*

692

Tanzania.　Staff list. 1964+ Dar es Salaam, Govt. Printer.　　　JQ3514.A32

693

Gt. Brit. *Colonial Office.*　Annual report on Zanzibar. 1946–[60?] London, H. M. Stationery Off. (*Its* Colonial annual reports)　　　　　　DT434.Z3G7

694

―――― Tanganyika under United Kingdom administration; report by Her Majesty's government . . . to the General Assembly of the United Nations. 1920–[60] London, H. M. Stationery Off.　　　　　　　　　　　　　J801.N15
　　　Title varies. Up to 1938, report made to the council of the League of Nations. No reports issued for 1939–46.

695

Handbook of Tanganyika. 2d ed. [Dar es Salaam, 1958] 703 p.　DT438.H3 1958
　　　First edition published in 1930.

696

Herrick, Allison B., *and others.*　Area handbook for Tanzania. Washington, U.S. Govt. Print. Off., 1968. xvi, 522 p.　　　　　　　　　　DT438.H4
　　　"DA pam. no. 550–62."

697

Morris-Hale, Walter.　British administration in Tanganyika from 1920 to 1945. With special references to the preparation of Africans for administrative positions. Genève, Imprimo, 1969 [c1968] 352 p.　　　　　JQ3315.A1M66

698

Sinitsyna, I. E.　Tanzaniiā. Partiiā i gosudarstvo. Moskva, "Nauka," 1972. 281 p.
　　　　　　　　　　　　　　　　　　　　　　　　JQ3519.A8T378
　　　Tanzania. Party and government.

699

Sperber, Klaus W. von・ Public administration in Tanzania. München, Weltforum Verlag [c1970] 120 p. (Afrika-Studien, Nr. 55)　　　　JQ3515.A1S63

700

Tanganyika.　Staff list. [?–1963] Dar es Salaam, Govt. Printer.　JQ3514.A3

701
Taylor, James C.   The political development of Tanganyika. Stanford, Calif., Stan-
    ford University Press, 1963. 254 p.   DT444.T3

702
Zanzibar.   Staff list. [1913–63] Zanzibar, Govt. Printer.   JQ2961.A43

THAILAND   [before 1939: SIAM]

703
Allison, Gordon H., *and* Auratai Smarnond.   Thailand's government (including
    dictionary-locator). Bangkok, Siam Security Brokers Co., 1972. 155 p.
                                                                       JQ1745.A64
        In three parts:—1. The Royal Thai government.—2. Dictionary-locator.—
    3. Decrees of the National Executive Council.

704
Bangkok, Thailand. Thammasat University. *Institute of Public Administration.*
    Thailand government organization manual series. Bangkok, 1959–[62] 11 v.
                                                                       JQ1745.B3
        Contents:—1. Public Health.—2. Agriculture.—3. Cooperatives.—4. Jus-
    tice.—5. Foreign Affairs.—6. Economic Affairs.—7. Communications.—8.
    Industry.—9. Finance.—10. Education.—11. Defence.

705
The Siam directory. 1947+ Bangkok, Thai Co. annual.   DS563.S53
        Includes a section on government organization.

706
Thailand official yearbook. 1964+ Bangkok, Govt. House Print. Off.   DS586.T5

707
Thailand year book. 1964/65+ Bangkok, Temple Publicity Services.   DS561.T57
        Includes a section on government organization.

───────────

708
The Directory for Bangkok and Siam. [1889–1941?] Bangkok, Bangkok Times Press.
                                                                       DS563.D5

709
Henderson, John W., *and others.*   Area handbook for Thailand. 3d revision. [Wash-
    ington, U.S. Govt. Print. Off.] 1971. xiv, 413 p.   DS571.H45 1971
    "DA pam. no. 550–53."

710
Kanchanadul, Prayoon.   L'organisation administrative de la Thaïlande (Siam).
    Paris, Rousseau, 1940. 200 p.   JQ1745.K3

711
Reeve, W. D.   Public administration in Siam. London, New York, Royal Institute
    of International Affairs [1951] 93 p.   JQ1742.R4

712
The Siam directory. 1st–? 1878–? Bangkok, Bangk'olém Office.   DS563.S5

713
Siffin, William J. The Thai bureaucracy: institutional change and development. Honolulu, East-West Center Press [1966] 291 p. JQ1745.A1S5

714
U.S. *Operations Mission to Thailand. Public Administration Division.* Organizational directory of the government of Thailand. 5th ed. [Bangkok] 1963. 142 p. JQ1744.U5
     Since 1970 the *Organizational Directory of the Government of Thailand* has been issued by the Translation and Secretarial Service, Bangkok.

715
Wales, Horace G. Q. Ancient Siamese government and administration. New York, Paragon Book Reprint Corp., 1965. 263 p. JQ1742.W3 1965
     First published in 1934.

TOGO

716
Togo. *Service du Protocole.* Liste officielle. [1961?+ Lomé] DLC

717
Togo. La République du Togo; note de documentation. Éd. provisoire. [Lomé?] 1959. 19 [i.e. 24] l. HC547.T6A46

718
Togo handbook. 1962–? [Lomé?] Information Service of the Govt. of Togo. DT582.8.A3

TONGA

719
Gt. Brit. *Colonial Office.* Tonga; a report. 1946–[62/63?] London, H. M. Stationery Off. (*Its* Colonial annual reports) DU880.A15
     From 1952/53, "List of members of the Privy Council, the Cabinet, and the Legislative Assembly" appears as an appendix.

720
Henderson, John W., *and others.* Area handbook for Oceania. [Washington, U.S. Govt. Print. Off.] 1971. xiv, 555 p. DU17.H45
     "DA pam. no. 550–94."
     Tonga: p. 202–204.

TRINIDAD AND TOBAGO

721
The Trinidad and Tobago year book. [v. 1+ 1866+] Port-of-Spain, Franklin's Electric Printery. F2121.T833

722
Gt. Brit. *Colonial Office.* Annual report on Trinidad and Tobago. 1946–[57?] London, H. M. Stationery Off. (*Its* Colonial annual reports) F2121.G8

TUNISIA

723
Bottin de la Tunisie. 1959+ Paris, Société Didot Bottin. annual.   HC547.T8B6

724
Administrative organization of Tunisia. [Tunis, 1944] 9 l.   JQ3327.A4 1944a
"Enclosure no. 1 to despatch no. 91, dated June 13, 1944, American Consulate, Tunis, Tunisia."

725
Annuaire tunisien du commerce, de l'industrie, de l'agriculture et des administrations de la régence. [1925–53?] Tunis, S. A. P. I.   JQ3327.A55

726
Debbasch, Charles. La République tunisienne. Paris, Librairie générale de droit et de jurisprudence [1962] 229 p. (Comment ils sont gouvernés, t. 6)   DT264.D4

727
Lambert, Paul. Nos corps élus. Tunis, En vente aux Bureaux du "Républicain" [1913] 180, xliv p.   JQ3327.L3

728
Le Franc, Jacques, of Tunis. Guide-memento du candidat à la fonction publique en Tunisie. Tunis, Éditions de la caravelle, c1953. 106 p.   JQ3323 1953.L4

729
Reese, Howard C., and others. Area handbook for the Republic of Tunisia. [Washington, U.S. Govt. Print. Off.] 1970. xvi, 415 p.   DT245.R4
"DA pam. no. 550–89."

TURKEY

730
Turkey. Merkezî Hükûmet Teşkilâtı Araştırma Projesi. Yönetim Kurulu. Merkezî hükûmet teşkilatı, kuruluş ve görevleri. Ankara [Türkiye ve Orta Doğu Âmme İdaresi Enstitüsü] 1963. 159 p.   JN9715 1963.A55 Orien Turk

731
—— Organization and functions of the central government of Turkey; report of the Managing Board of the Central Government Organization Research Project. Ankara [Public Administration Institute for Turkey and the Middle East] 1965. 408 p.   JN9715 1963.A5513
Translation of Merkezî hükûmet teşkilâtı, kuruluş ve görevleri.

732
—— T. C. devlet teşkilâtı rehberi. Ankara [Türkiye ve Orta Doğu Âmme İdaresi Enstitüsü] 1963. 669 p.   JN9721.A45 Orien Turk

733
—— Turkish government organization manual. Ankara [Public Administration Institute for Turkey and the Middle East, 1966] 572 p.   JN9721.A4513
Translation of T. C. devlet teşkilâtı rehberi.

734

Conk, A. Cemil, *and* Namik K. Savun. Turkish public administration; a report on the rationalization of the state organization. Bloomington, Institute of Training for Public Service, Dept. of Govt., Indiana University, 1961. 129 l. (Selected papers on public administration, no. 1) JN9731.C6

Translation of an unpublished report, Dec. 1950, presented to the Turkish Prime Minister's Office.

735

Dalmış, Doğan. Turkish government organization manual, 1959. Ankara [1959] 187 p. JN9731.D34

736

Dodd, Clement H. Politics and government in Turkey. Manchester, Manchester University Press, 1969. xvi, 335 p. JN9715 1969.D6

737

Gorvine, Albert, *and* Laurence L. Barber, Jr. Organization and functions of Turkish ministries. Ankara, Ajans-Türk Matbaasi, 1957. 212 p. (Ankara University. Faculty of Political Sciences' publications, no. 73:55) DLC LL

738

Hanusets', Oleksandr I. Derz͡havnyĭ ustriĭ Turechchyny v period respubliky. Kyïv, Vyd-vo Akademiï nauk Ukr. RSR, 1961. 94 p. JN9711.H2

Turkish government organization during the republic.

739

Milliyet 1970 [i.e. bin dokuz üyz yetmiş. İstanbul, Milliyet Yayın Ltd. Şti Yayınları, 1971] 368 p. (Milliyet'ten secmeler dizisi, 2) D410.5 1970.M54 Orien Turk

Yearbook of the newspaper Milliyet.

740

Öztürk Kâzim, *comp.* Türkiye Cumhuriyeti hükumetleri vs programları. İstanbul [Ak Yayınları] 1968. xiv, 670 p. (Ak Yayınları Limited Şirketi neşriyatı, 16) JN9711.O48 Orien Turk

Governments of the Turkish Republic and their programs.

741

Roberts, Thomas D., *and others.* Area handbook for the Republic of Turkey. Washington, U.S. Govt. Print. Off., 1970. xvi, 438 p. DR417.R54

"DA pam. no. 550–59."

742

Sturm, Albert L., *and others.* Bibliography on public administration in Turkey, 1928–1957; selective and annotated. Ankara, 1959. 224 p. (Faculty of Political Sciences. University of Ankara. Faculty publication 88–70) Z7165.T9S7

743

Ticaret yıllığı. Annuaire commercial. [1868]+ İstanbul. DR413.T5

Title varies.

Vols. for 1868–1922/23 included section on central government.

744

Türkiye Cumhuriyeti devlet yıllığı. [1929]+ [Ankara?]

AY1038.T8T8 Orien Turk

Government yearbook.

Vols. for 1842?–1927/28 issued under the title *Salnāme.*

UGANDA

745
Uganda government directory. [July 1963]+ Entebbe.   DLC
    Earlier title (1956–63), *Central Government Organisation.* Until 1965
    issued as a supplement to *Uganda Gazette.* Frequency varies.

746
Gt. Brit. *Colonial Office.* Uganda; report for the year. 1946–[61?] London, H. M.
    Stationery Off. (*Its* Colonial annual reports)   DT434.U2G57

747
Gt. Brit. *Naval Intelligence Division.* A handbook of the Uganda Protectorate.
    London, H. M. Stationery Off. [1920] 447 p.   DT434.U2G6 1920

748
Herrick, Allison B., *and others.* Area handbook for Uganda. Washington, U.S.
    Govt. Print. Off., 1969. xvi, 456 p.   DT434.U2H4
    "DA pam. no. 550–74."

749
Uganda. The handbook of Uganda. 2d ed. By H. R. Wallis. London, Published
    for the Govt. of the Uganda Protectorate by the Crown Agents for the colonies,
    1920. xxi, 316 p.   DT434.U2A5 1920
    First edition was published in 1913.

750
Uganda. Staff list. [1941?]+ Entebbe, Govt. Printer.   JQ2951.A43

751
Uganda. *Ministry of Information, Broadcasting and Tourism.* Facts about Uganda.
    [Kampala?] 1968. 106 p.   DT434.U2A35

752
_____ Uganda, 1962–1963. Entebbe, Govt. Printer, 1964. 233 p.   HC517.U2A54

753
Uganda. [1964]+ Entebbe, Govt. Printer.   DT434.U2A33

754
Uganda trade directory, including classified trade index. 1966–67+ London, Diplo-
    matic Press and Pub. Co.   HF3899.U5U55

UNION OF SOVIET SOCIALIST REPUBLICS

755
Ananov, Iosif N. Ministerstva v SSSR. Moskva, Gos. izd-vo i͡urid. lit-ry. 1960.
    286 p.   JN6542.A7

756
Davitnidze, Igor' L. Kollegii ministerstv. (Pravovoe polozhenie i organizaci͡ia
    raboty.) Moskva, I͡Urid. lit., 1972. 152 p.   DLC LL

757
Directory of Soviet officials. [n. p.] 1966+ 2 v. (looseleaf)   JN6521.D5
    Contents:—v. 1. USSR and RSFSR.—v. 2. Union republics.

758
Hazard, John N.   The Soviet system of government. 4th ed. rev. Chicago, University of Chicago Press [1968] 275 p.   JN6518.H3 1968

759
Hodnett, Grey, *and* Val Ogareff.   Leaders of the Soviet Republics, 1955–1972: a guide to posts and occupants. Canberra, Dept. of Political Science, Research School of Social Sciences, Australian National University, 1973. xix, 454 p.
                                                                        JN6521.H62

760
Institut zur Erforschung der UdSSR.   Key officials of the government. [2d ed. Compiled by S. I. Melinska] Munich, Institute for the Study of the USSR, Biographic Section, 1966. 2 v. (*Its* [Issledovaniia i materialy] Series 2. no. 93–94)
                                                                        JN6521.I6 1966
       First edition was published in 1962.

761
——— Party and government officials of the Soviet Union, 1917–1967. Compiled by the Institute for the Study of the USSR, Munich, Germany. Metuchen, N. J., Scarecrow Press [1969] 214 p.   JN6598.K7I54

762
Keefe, Eugene K., *and others.*   Area handbook for the Soviet Union. [Washington, U.S. Govt. Print. Off.] 1971. xviii, 827 p.   DK18.K43
       "DA pam. no. 550–95."

763
Pravovoe polozhenie ministerstv SSSR. Moskva, IUrid. lit., 1971. 296 p.   DLC LL
       Legal basis of ministries in the USSR.

764
Raymond, Ellsworth L.   The Soviet state. New York, Macmillan [1968] xv, 462 p.
                                                                        DK266.R378

765
Sluzhashchii sovetskogo gosudarstvennogo apparata. Moskva, IUrid. lit., 1970. 278 p.
                                                                        DLC LL
       Employees of the Soviet government apparatus.

766
Soviet political leaders. Nov. 30, 1955–? [n. p.]   JN6521.S55

767
U.S. *Central Intelligence Agency.*   Directory of Ukrainian officials. [Washington] 1973. 195 p. (Reference aid)   JN6599.U4U54

768
U.S. *Dept. of State. Division of Biographic Information.*   Personnel in the Communist Party, government and mass organizations of the U.S.S.R. and the 15 Soviet Republics. [Washington] 1958+ 1 v. (looseleaf) (*Its* Biographic directory, BD no. 253/1)   DR5.U55 no. 253/1

769
Wesson, Robert G.   The Soviet state: an aging revolution. New York, Wiley [1972] 222 p.   JN6515 1972.W472

For imperial, pre-1917 Russia, the following directories will be of assistance.

770
Adres-kalendar.   Obshchaĭa rospis' nachal'stvuĭushchikh i prochikh dolzhostnykh lits po vsiem upravleniām Rossiiskoĭ Imperia. [1849–1915] Sanktpeterburg.
JN6521.A2
Microfilm 22270 JN
     Directory of high officials of the Russian Empire.

771
Spisok vysshim chinam gosudarstvennago, gubernskago i eparkhial'nago upravleniĭ. [Sanktpeterburg] 1849–1916.   JN6521.S7
     List of high officials of the central and regional governments and of the ecclesiastical organization.

UNITED ARAB EMIRATES   (Formerly Trucial States. Includes: Abu Dhabi, Ajman, Dubai, Fujaira, Ras al Khaima, Sharja, and Umm al Qaiwan)

772
Stanford Research Institute. Area handbook for the Peripheral States of the Arabian Peninsula. Prepared for the American University. [Washington, U.S. Govt. Print. Off.] 1971. xiv, 201 p.   DS247.A14S78
     "DA pam. no. 550–92."
     The Gulf States; p. 125–152.

UNITED STATES OF AMERICA

773
United States government manual. 1973/74+ [Washington] Office of the Federal Register [U.S. Govt. Print. Off.] annual.   JK421.A3
     Began publication in 1935.
     Title varies: 1935–48, *United States Government Manual*; 1949–72/73, *United States Government Organization Manual* (1962/63–63/64, *U.S. Government Organization Manual*).

774
U.S. *Congress.*   Official congressional directory. [1809]+ Washington, U.S. Govt. Print. Off. annual.   JK1011

775
U.S. *Congress. Senate. Committee on Government Operations.*   Organization of federal executive departments and agencies; report. Dec. 31, 1946+ [Washington, U.S. Govt. Print. Off.]   JK646.A3
     Reports accompanied by a diagram. Since 1970, only the diagram is issued.

776
U.S. Government organization chart manual. 1973+ Columbus, Ohio, Symetics Group Inc. 1 v. (looseleaf)

777
American register, or Blue book . . . containing the names of the principal civil officers of the federal government; army and navy list, etc. New York, J. Disturnell [1849?–77]   JK6.A5

778
Brookings Institution, *Washington, D. C. Institute for Government Research.*   Service
monographs of the United States government. no. 1–[66] Washington, 1919–
[34]   JK421.A1B6 (3d set)
    Reprinted in 1974 by AMS Press, New York.

779
Encyclopedia of governmental advisory organizations. no. 1+ July 1973+ Detroit,
Gale Research Co. quarterly.   JK468.C7E5

780
Mosher, Robert B.   Executive register of the United States 1789–1902. Washington,
Govt. Print. Off., 1905. 351 p. ([U.S.] 58th Cong., 3d sess. Senate. Doc. no.
196)   JK661 1902a

781
Praeger library of U.S. government departments and agencies.

1. Pizer, Vernon.   The United States Army. (1967. 213 p.   UA25.P5)
2. Fitch, Edwin M.   The Alaska railroad. (1967. 326 p.   HE2791.A38)
3. Huston, Luther A.   The Department of Justice. (1967. 270 p.   KF5107.H8)
4. MacCloskey, Monro.   The United States Air Force. (1967. 244 p.
   UG633.M219)
5. Burkhardt, Robert.   The Federal Aviation Administration. (1967. 249 p.
   HE9803.A4B8)
6. Donovan, James A.   The United States Marine Corps. (1967. 246 p.
   VE23.D65)
7. Moore, Ernest G.   The Agricultural Research Service. (1967. 244 p.
   S21.C9M6)
8. Popkin, Roy.   The Environmental Science Services Administration. (1967. 278 p.
   QC875.U7P6)
9. Willmann, John B.   The Department of Housing and Urban Development.
   (1967. 207 p.   HT175.U6W48)
10. Cullinan, Gerald.   The Post Office Department. (1967. 272 p.   HE6371.C85)
    Cullinan, Gerald.   The United States Postal Service. (1973. 271 p.
    HE6371.C86)
11. Borklund, Carl W.   The Department of Defense. (1968. 342 p.   UA23.6.B58)
12. Carrison, Daniel J.   The United States Navy. (1968. 262 p.   VA55.C3)
13. Clague, Ewan.   The Bureau of Labor Statistics. (1968. 271 p.   HD8051.A9L3)
14. Henderson, John W.   The United States Information Agency. (1969. 324 p.
    E744.5.H4)
15. Parris, Addison W.   The Small Business Administration. (1968. 292 p.
    HG3729.U5P28)
16. Schaffter, Dorothy.   The National Science Foundation. (1969. 278 p.
    Q11.U84S3)
17. Marvell, Thomas B.   The Federal Home Loan Bank Board. (1969. 291 p.
    HG2040.0.U5M37)
18. Blancké, W. Wendell.   The Foreign Service of the United States.   (1969. 286 p.
    JX1705.B5)
19. Harvey, Donald R.   The Civil Service Commission. (1970. 233 p.
    JK691.H32)
20. Brundage, Percival F.   The Bureau of the Budget, (1970. 327 p.   HJ2052.B75)
21. Oehser, Paul H.   The Smithsonian Institution. (1970. 275 p.   Q11.S8O39)
22. Carey, Robert G.   The Peace Corps. (1970. 274 p.   HC60.5.C34)
23. Simms, Denton H.   The Soil Conservation Service. (1970. 238 p.   S622.S44)
24. Fitch, Edwin M., *and* John M. Shanklin.   The Bureau of Outdoor Recreation.
    (1970. 227 p.   GV53.F48)

25. Chommie, John C.   The Internal Revenue Service. (1970. 267 p.
  HJ5018.C45)
26. Kling, Robert E.   The Government Printing Office. (1970. 242 p.
  Z232.U6K57)
27. Clawson, Marion.   The Bureau of Land Management. (1971. 209 p.
  HD181.G8C57)
28. Wagner, Susan.   The Federal Trade Commission. (1971. 261 p.
  HD2795.W18)
29. Jones, Stacy V.   The Patent Office. (1971. 234 p.   KF3120.J64)
30. Frome, Michael.   The Forest Service. (1971. 24 p.   SD565.F7)
31. Everhart, William C.   The National Park Service. (1972. 276 p. SB482.A4E95)
32. Rasmussen, Wayne D., *and* Gladys L. Baker.   The Department of Agriculture.
  (1972. 257 p.   S21.C9R37)
33. Eckler, A. Ross.   The Bureau of the Census. (1972. 268 p.   HA37.U55E25)
34. Warne, William E.   The Bureau of Reclamation. (1973. 270 p.   TC823.W37)
35. Owen, Marguerite.   The Tennessee Valley Authority. (1973. 275 p.
  TK1425.M8O93)
36. Hirsch, Richard, *and* Joseph J. Trento.   The National Aeronautics and Space
  Administration. (1973. 245 p.   TL789.8.U5H55)
37. Grossman, Jonathan Ph.   The Department of Labor. (1973. 309 p.
  HD4835.U4G76)
38. Goodrum, Charles A.   The Library of Congress. (1974. 292 p.   Z733.U6G66)
39. Miles, Rufus E.   The Department of Health, Education and Welfare. (1974.
  326 p.   RA5.M54)
40. Van Cleve, Ruth G.   The Office of Territorial Affairs. (1974. 226 p.
  JK2556.V32)
41. McCulloch, Frank W., *and* Tim Bornstein.   The National Labor Relations
  Board. (1974. 200 p.   KF3372.M23)
42. Allardice, Corbin, *and* Edward R. Trapnell.   The Atomic Energy Commission.
  (1974. 236 p.   HD9698.U52A63)
[43. Estes, Thomas S., *and* Edwin A. Lightner.   The Department of State. (Sched-
  uled for publication in 1975)]

782
U.S. *Civil Service Commission.*   Official register of the United States. [1816–1959]
  Washington, U.S. Govt. Print. Off.   JK5
    Vols. 1816–60, issued by the U.S. Dept. of State; 1861–1905, by the U.S.
    Dept. of the Interior; 1907–32 by the Bureau of the Census; 1933–59, by
    the U.S. Civil Service Commission.
    Biennial, 1861–1921; annual, 1923–59.
    Title varies: 1816–77, *Register of Officers and Agents, Civil, Military and
    Naval.*

783
U.S. *Congress.*   The United States congressional directories, 1789–1840. [Edited
  by Perry M. Goldman and James S. Young] New York, Columbia University
  Press, 1973.   JK1011.U53

784
U.S. *Congress. House. Committee on Government Operations.*   Replies from executive departments and federal agencies to inquiry regarding use of advisory committees (January 1, 1953 to January 1, 1956) Washington, U.S. Govt. Print.
  Off., 1956–?   JK468.C7A516
    Contents.—pt. 1. Department of Agriculture.—pt. 2. Department of Com-
    merce.—pt. 3. Department of Health, Education, and Welfare.—pts. 4–5.
    Department of Defense.—pt. 6. Department of the Interior. Department of
    Justice. Department of Labor. Post Office Department. Department of State.
    Treasury Department.

785
U.S. *National Emergency Council.* Current organization charts of United States administrative agencies. [Washington, U.S. Govt. Print. Off., 1934] 1 v. (loose-leaf)   JK421.A4 1934

786
_____ Daily revised manual of emergency recovery agencies and facilities provided by the United States government. [Washington, U.S. Govt. Print. Off., 1934] 1 v. (looseleaf)   JK421.A28
   Superseded by the *United States Government Manual,* 1935+.

787
U.S. *President.* Federal advisory committees; annual report of the President to the Congress, including data on individual committees. 1st+ 1973+ Washington, Subcommittee on Budgeting, Management, and Expenditures, U.S. Govt. Print. Off.   JK468.C7U57a

788
Wynkoop, Sally, *and* David W. Parish. Directories of government agencies. Rochester, N. Y., Libraries Unlimited, 1969. 242 p.   Z7165.U5W9

UPPER VOLTA

789
Encyclopédie africaine et malgache. [Haute Volta] Paris, Larousse [1964] 30, 464 p.   DT553.U7E5
   General encyclopedia preceded by a section devoted to the Republic of
◄ Upper Volta.

790
Lippens, Philippe. La République de Haute Volta. Paris, Berger-Levrault, 1972. 62 p. (Encyclopédie politique et constitutionnelle. Série Afrique)
                                                                  JQ3398.A3 1972.L5

URUGUAY

791
Anuario "El Siglo," guía general de la República Oriental del Uruguay. [Montevideo] "Casa A. Barreiro y Ramos."   F2704.5.A5
   Publication began in 1863 under title *Almanaque-guía de el Siglo* (F2701.A44). The so-called 3d series of *Anuario* issued 1940–52?

792
"Guía nacional" de la República Oriental del Uruguay. [1901–?] Montevideo.
                                                                     F2704.5.G94

793
Oddone, Juan A. Tablas cronológicas: poder ejecutivo, poder legislativo, 1830–1967. [2. ed. corr. y aumentada] Montevideo, Universidad de la República Oriental del Uruguay, Facultad de Humanidades y Ciencias, 1967. 190 p. (Instituto de Investigaciones Históricas. Manuales auxiliares para la investigación histórica, no. 1)   JL3621.A2O3 1967
   First edition published in 1955 under the title *Poder ejecutivo, poder legislativo, 1830–1951: tablas cronológicas.* (JL3621.O3)

794
Weil, Thomas E., *and others*. Area handbook for Uruguay. [Washington, U.S. Govt. Print. Off.] 1971. xiv, 439 p.   HN353.5.W45
"DA pam. no. 550–97."

VENEZUELA

795
Venezuela. *Comisión de Administración Pública.* Directorio de la administración pública nacional; contiene dirección, teléfono y nómina de personal directivo de ministerios, institutos autónomos, empresas del Estado, fondos patrimoniales y otros organismos públicos. [Caracas] 1967. 78 p.   JL3821.A3 1967

796
———— Manual de organización; base legal, atribuciones, estructura y funciones del poder ejecutivo. [Caracas] 1966. xxiv, 605 p.   JL3842.A48 1966
Earlier edition published in 1963.

797
Calendario manual y guía universal de forasteros en Venezuela para el año 1810. Estudio preliminar por Pedro Grases. Caracas, Academia Nacional de la Historia, 1959. 155 p. (Biblioteca de la Academia Nacional de la Historia, 16)
F2322.C3

798
Indicador de Caracas y de la república. 1919/1920–? Caracas, Litografía del Comercio.   F2304.5.I39

799
International Bureau of the American Republics, *Washington, D.C.* Venezuela [a handbook] [Washington, Govt. Print. Off., 1892] 199 p. (*Its* Bulletin, no. 34. February 1892)   F1403.I68 no. 34
F2308.I61

800
———— Venezuela [a handbook] [Washington, Govt. Print. Off., 1899] 2 v. (*Its* Bulletin, no. 93. Rev. ed. 1899)   F1403.I68 no. 93
F2308.I62
In English and Spanish.

801
———— Venezuela. Esbozo geográfico, recursos naturales, legislación, condiciones económicas, desarrollo alcanzado, prospecto de futuro desenvolvimiento. Ed. y comp. para Oficina Internacional de las Repúblicas Americanas por N. Veloz Goiticoa, 1904. Caracas, Impr. Bolívar, 1905. 695 p.   F2308.I64

802
———— Venezuela. Geographical sketch, natural resources, laws, economic conditions, actual development, prospects of future growth. Ed. and comp. for the International Bureau of the American Republics by N. Veloz Goiticoa, 1904. Washington, Govt. Print. Off., 1904 608 p.   F2308.I63
Another issue published as House Doc. 145, pt. 3, 58th Cong., 3 sess. (F2308.I632).

803
Landaeta Rosales, Manuel. Gobiernos de Venezuela desde 1810 hasta 1905. Caracas, Tip. Herrera Irigoyen & Ca., 1905. 112 p.   JL3824.L3

804

El Primer libro impreso en Venezuela, por Pedro Grases. Edición facsimilar del Calendario manual y guía universal de forasteros en Venezuela para el año de 1810. Caracas, Ministerio de Educación, Dirección de Cultura y Bellas Artes, 1952. 100 p. (Biblioteca venezolana de cultura. Colección "Andrés Bello")
F2322.P7

805

La Reforma administrativa en Venezuela (1969–1971). Caracas, Comisión de Administración Pública, 1971. 160 l.   JL3831.R4
"Publicación preparada para el Seminario Interregional de las Naciones Unidas sobre Reformas Administrativas en Gran Escala en los Paises en Desarrollo (Londres, 25 de octubre–2 de noviembre de 1971)"

806

Venezuela. *Comisión de Administración Pública.* Informe sobre la reforma de la administración pública nacional. Caracas, 1972. 2 v.   JL3831.A45
Appendixes following each section of the report contain documents and legislation. Includes charts of agencies.

807

Venezuela. 1955–? Caracas, Ministerio de Relaciones Exteriores.   F2308.V4
Includes lists of government agencies.

808

Venezuela.   [Lima] Latín América [1963?] 1 v. (looseleaf)   F2304.5.V4
Includes a section on government organization.

809

Weil, Thomas E., *and others.* Area handbook for Venezuela. [Washington, U.S. Govt. Print. Off.] 1971. xiv, 525 p.   F2308.W4 1971
"DA pam. no. 550–71."
Revision of 1964 edition.

VIETNAM

810

Annuaire général, administratif, commercial et industriel de l'Indochine. [1887–1939/40?] Hanoi-Haiphong, Impr. d'Extrême Orient.   DS532.A5
Title varies.

811

Dăng-Phu'o'ng-Nghi.   Les institutions publiques du Viet-Nam au XVIIIe siècle. Paris, École française d'Extrême Orient. 1969. 145 p. (Publications de l'École française d'Extrême Orient, v. 64)   JQ811.D34

812

France. *Haut Commissariat de France en Indochine.* Annuaire administratif des services communs. [1947–?] Saigon.   JQ821.A3

813

Galembert, J. de.   Les administrations et les services publics indochinois. 2. éd., rev. et augm., par E. Erard. Hanoi, Impr. Mac-Dinh-Tu, Le-Van-Tan succr, 1931. xxiv, 1,023 p.   JQ831.G3 1931

814
Southard, Betty J.   Provisional government of Viet Nam since 1945. Columbus, Ohio,
    Capital Properties [1951?)] 57 1.   JQ811.56

VIETNAM, DEMOCRATIC REPUBLIC OF

815
Budanov, Anatoliĭ G.   Gosudarstvennyĭ stroĭ Demokraticheskoĭ Respubliki V'etnam.
    Moskva, Gos. izd-vo ĭurid. lit-ry, 1958. 108 p. (Gosudarstvennyĭ stroĭ stran mira)
                                                                         JQ815.B8
    Government organization of the Democratic Republic of Vietnam.

816
Fall, Bernard B.   Le Viet-Minh, la République démocratique du Viet-Nam, 1945–
    1960. Paris, A. Colin, 1960. 376 p. (Cahiers de la Fondation nationale des
    sciences politiques, 106)   H31.F6 no. 106

817
_____ The Viet-Minh regime; government and administration in the Democratic
    Republic of Vietnam. Rev. and enl. ed. Issued jointly with the Southeast Asia
    Program, Cornell University. New York, Institute of Pacific Relations, 1956.
    196 p.   JQ815.F3 1956

818
Mazaev, Al'bert G.   Gosudarstvennyĭ stroĭ Demokraticheskoĭ Respubliki V'etnam.
    Moskva, Gos, izd-vo ĭurid. lit-ry, 1963. 84 p. (Gosudarstvennyĭ stroĭ stran
    mira)   JQ815 1963.M3
    Government organization of the Democratic Republic of Vietnam.

819
Merzlĭakov, Nikolaĭ S.   Demokraticheskaĭa Respublika V'etnam; gosudarstvennyĭ
    stroĭ. Moskva, 1961. 191 p.   JQ815 1961.M4
    Issued by the Institut mezhdunarodnykh otnosheniĭ.

820
Smith, Harvey H., and others.   Area handbook for North Vietnam. Washington,
    U.S. Govt. Print. Off., 1967. 494 p.   DS557.A7S57
    "DA pam. no. 550–57."
    Earlier editions published under the title Area Handbook for Vietnam and
    entered under American University, Washington, D.C., Foreign Areas Studies
    Division (DS557.A5A72). They cover both North and South Vietnam.

VIETNAM, REPUBLIC OF

821
Saigon. Học-viện Quốc-gia Hành-chánh.   Niên-giám hành-chánh. [1971] Saigon.
    443 p.   JQ831.S2 Orien Viet
    Government organization manual.

822
_____ Viet Nam government organization manual, 1957–58. Saigon, National Insti-
    tute of Administration, Research and Documentation Division, 1958. xv, 275 p.
                                                                         JQ831.S23
_____ _____ Supplement. Saigon, 1960. 174 1.   JQ831.S23 Suppl.

823
Annuaire général du Vietnam. Tông niên giám Việt-Nam. General directory of
Vietnam. 1952/53–? Saigon, A. V. T., Bureaux d'études techniques et écono-
miques. DS557.A5A18

824
The Cabinet of Prime Minister Nguyen Van Loc; activities in the past six months
(Nov. 9, 1967–May 9, 1968). [Saigon] Prime Minister's Press Office [1968]
118 p. JQ826 1968.C22

825
Kuo, Shou-hua. Yüeh, Liao, Chien san kuo t'ung chien. Directory of Viet-nam, Laos
and Cambodia. Taipei, Central Cultural Supply Agency [1966] 18, 6, 320 p.
DS532.5.K86 Orien China

826
Michigan. State University, *East Lansing. Vietnam Advisory Group, Saigon.* Report
on the organization of the Department of Agriculture [Department of Educa-
tion, Department of Land Registration and Agrarian Reform, Department of
Information and Youth and Sports, Department of National Economy and the
Special Commissariat for Civic Action. Saigon?] 1956–57. 6 v. JQ831.M5

827
Nghiem-Dang. Viet-Nam; politics and public administration. Honolulu, East-West
Center Press [c1966] 437 p. JQ831.N46

828
Smith, Harvey H., *and others.* Area handbook for South Vietnam. Washington,
U.S. Govt. Print. Off., 1967. xiv, 510 p. DS557.A5S575 1967
"DA pam. no. 550–55."
Earlier editions published under the title *Area Handbook for Vietnam* and
entered under American University, Washington, D.C., Foreign Areas Studies
Division (DS557.A5A72). They cover both North and South Vietnam.

829
Thành tích tám năm hoạt động cúa chánh phú: 1954–1962. Saigon, 1962. 1072 p.
JQ826 1962.T45 Orien Viet
Report on activities of the government during 8 years. Similar reports
published for 1954–58, 1954–60, and 1954–61.

830
U.S. *AID Mission in Vietnam. Public Administration Division.* Public administration bulletin Vietnam. [1963–? Saigon] irregular. JQ801.U45

831
Vietnam. *Service du protocole.* Liste des personalités résidant sur le territoire de
Saigon-Giadịnh. [October 1957] Saigon. 57 p.

WESTERN SAMOA

832
Davidson, James W. Samoa mo Samoa; the emergence of the independent state
of Western Samoa. Melbourne, New York, Oxford University Press, 1967.
467 p. DU819.A2D3

833
Henderson, John W., *and others.* Area handbook for Oceania. [Washington, U.S.
    Govt. Print. Off.] 1971. xiv, 555 p.   DU17.H45
    "DA pam. no. 550–94."
    Western Samoa: p. 196–200.

834
Western Samoa. Handbook of Western Samoa. Wellington, W. A. G. Skinner,
    Govt. Printer, 1925. 174 p.   DU819.A2A5 1925
    "Government departments": p [74]–100.

835
Western Samoa. Mandated territory of Western Samoa; [report of the government
    of New Zealand on the administration of] 1920/21–[58/59?] Wellington?
                                                                  J981.S3N33

YEMEN ARAB REPUBLIC

836
Kotlov, Lev N. Ĭemenskaĭa Arabskaĭa Respublika. (Spravochnik). Moskva, "Nauka,"
    1971. 287 p.   DS247.Y4K68
    Issued by the Institut vostokovedenia of the Academy of Sciences.

837
Orlov, Evengiĭ A. Gosudarstvennyĭ stroĭ Ĭemena. Moskva, Gos. izd-vo ĭurid. lit-ry,
    1958. 29 p. (Gosudarstvennyĭ stroĭ stran mira)   JQ1825.Y4O7
    Government organization of Yemen.

838
Stanford Research Institute. Area handbook for the Peripheral States of the Arabian
    Peninsula. Prepared for the American University. [Washington, U.S. Govt.
    Print. Off.] 1971. xiv, 201 p.   DS247.A14S78
    "DA pam. no. 550–92."
    Yemen: p. 35–64.

YEMEN, PEOPLE'S DEMOCRATIC REPUBLIC OF

839
Aden. Administration report of Aden. [1908?–58] Delhi.   J605.R3

840
Aden. Staff list. [1948–66? Aden]   JQ745.A3A4

841
The Aden who's who and official directory. [Steamer Point. 1933?–?] semiannual.
                                                                  DS247.A2A25

842
Brinton, Jasper Y. Aden and the Federation of South Arabia. Washington, Ameri-
    can Society of International Law [1964] 81 p. (An occasional paper of the
    American Society of International Law)   DS247.A28B7

843
Gt. Brit. *Colonial Office.* Annual report on Aden and Aden Protectorate. 1946–
[57/58?] London, H. M. Stationery Off. (*Its* Colonial annual reports)
DS249.A2A35

844
Stanford Research Institute. Area handbook for the Peripheral States of the
Arabian Peninsula. Prepared for the American University. [Washington, U.S.
Govt. Print. Off.] 1971. xiv, 201 p.   DS247.A14S78
"DA pam. no. 550–92."
People's Republic of Southern Yemen: p. 65–94.

YUGOSLAVIA

845
Adresar saveznih državnih organa i ustanova. [1953–?] Beograd, Novinska ustanova
"Službeni list FNRJ."   JN9667.A25
Directory of federal government agencies and institutions.

846
Directory of Yugoslav officials. [n. p.] 1970. 216 p.   JN9667.D55

847
Društveno-političke zajednice. Beograd, "Međunarodna štampa-Interpress," 1968. 4 v.
JN9667.D7
A directory of social and political institutions.
Contents.—t. 1. Federation.—t. 2. Socialist republics and autonomous
regions.—t. 3–4. Communes.

848
Državni kalendar kraljevine Srba, Hrvata i Slovenaca. [1919–24?] Beograd.
DR364.D7
Official calendar of the Kingdom of the Serbs, Croats, and Slovenes.

849
Državni kalendar Kraljevine Srbije. [1853–1914] Beograd, Izd. Državne štamparije.
JN9647.D7
Official calendar of the Kingdom of Serbia.

850
A Handbook of Yugoslavia. Belgrade, "Review," the Yugoslav Illustrated Magazine,
[1969] 285 p.   DR305.H3

851
Kraljevina Srba, Hrvata i Slovenaca; almanah. [1921/22–?] Zagreb. annual (irreg-
ular)   DR301.K7
The Kingdom of the Serbs, Croats, and Slovenes; almanac.

852
Telegrafska agencija Nova Jugoslavija. *Dokumentacija.* Political and business guide
of Yugoslavia. Beograd. Tanjug, 1967. 6, 145, 21 p.   JN9667.T4

853

——— Politički i poslovni imenik. Beograd, Tanjug, 1969. 7, 38 p.   JN9667.T43
A directory of federal and regional officials. Latest edition published in
1972.

854

U.S. *Central Intelligence Agency.* Directory of Yugoslav officials. [Washington]
1972. 297 p. (Reference aid)   JN9667.U54 1972
Previous editions were issued without author or publisher statement and
are entered under title (see above).

855

Yugoslavia. *Savezna skupština.* Organizaciona struktura Savezne skupštine, Savez-
nog izvršnog veća i ostalih organa federacije. Beograd, Sekretarijat za informativnu službu Jugoslavije; "Prosveta," 1967. 75 p. (Biblioteka Savezne skupštine,
kolo 4, sv. 5)   JN9673.A53

856

——— ——— Beograd [Prosveta; Sekretarijat za informativnu službu Savezne
skupštine] 1969. 92 p. (Biblioteka Savezne skupštine, kolo 6, sv. 5)
                                                                JN9673.A53 1969
Organizational structure of the Federal Assembly, Supreme Federal Council,
and other federal agencies.

For the government in exile and the provisional national government
in occupied Yugoslavia (1941–45), see:

857

Carnegie Endowment for International Peace. *Library.* European governments in
exile. Compiled by Helen L. Scanlon. [Washington, 1943] 24 p. (*Its* Memoranda
series, no. 3. Revised January 25, 1943)   JX1906.A35 no. 3a

858

United Committee of South-Slavs in London. New Yugoslavia. London, The United
South Slav Committee [1944] 36 p.   D742.Y8U5
Contents.—The new Yugoslavia.—Declaration and decisions of the Anti-
fascist Council in Jajce on November 29–30, 1943.—Composition of the
Provisional National Government.—Parliamentary debates, House of Com-
mons.—Mr. Churchill's speech.

ZAÏRE [before 1971: CONGO]

859

Annuaire de la République démocratique du Congo. [1965?+ Kinshasa] Havas
Congo Kin.   HC591.C6A635

860

Annuaire du Congo Belge; administratif, commercial, industriel et agricole. Livre
d'adresses. [1902–58/59?] Bruxelles.   DT643.A5

861

Belgium. *Ministère des affaires africaines.* Annuaire officiel. Officieel jaarboek.
[1910–59?] Bruxelles.   JQ3607.A3

862
Belgium. *Office de l'information et des relations publiques pour le Congo belge et le Ruanda-Urundi.* Belgian Congo. [Translated from the French] Brussels, 1959–60. 2 v.   DT644.A4853

863
––––––– Le Congo belge. Bruxelles, 1958–59. 2 v.   DT644.A485

864
Centre de recherche et d'information sociopolitiques. Congo. 1959+ Bruxelles. (*Its* Dossiers)   DT641.C43

865
Encyclopédie du Congo Belge. Bruxelles, Bieleveld [1950–52] 3 v.   DT643.E5
       Institutions politiques, administratives et judiciaries, v. 3: p. 515–554.

866
Halewyck de Heusch, Michel.   Les institutions politiques et administratives des pays africains soumis à l'autorité de la Belgique. Bruxelles, Impr. Bolyn [1938] 54 p.
                                                                                  JQ3604.H3

867
McDonald, Gordon C., *and others.* Area handbook for the Democratic Republic of the Congo (Congo Kinshasa). [Washington, U.S. Govt. Print. Off.] 1971. xviii, 587 p.   DT644.M24
       "DA pam. no. 550–67."

868
Mpinga-Kasenda.   L'administration publique du Zaïre; l'impact du milieu socio-politique sur sa structure et son fonctionnement. Paris, Pedone [1973] 316 p. (Institut d'études politiques de Bordeaux. Centre d'étude d'Afrique noire: Série Afrique noire, 3)   HC501.S4 no. 3

ZAMBIA   [before 1964: NORTHERN RHODESIA]

869
Gt. Brit. *Colonial Office.* Annual report on Northern Rhodesia. 1946–[62?] London, H. M. Stationery Off. (*Its* Colonial annual reports)   DT963.A3

870
Kaplan, Irving, *and others.* Area handbook for Zambia. Washington, U.S. Govt. Print. Off., 1969. xvi, 482 p.   DT963.K26
       "DA pam. no. 550–75."

871
Mulford, David C. Zambia: the politics of independence, 1957–1964. London Oxford University Press, 1967. 362 p.   JQ2811.M8

872
Rhodesia, Northern. *Information Dept.* Government ministries in Northern Rhodesia. 1959. 4 p.   DLC

873
––––––– The Northern Rhodesia handbook. [Lusaka] 1953. 263 p.   DT963.A5 1953
       Earlier editions published in 1938, 1948, and 1950.

874
Rhodesia and Nyasaland. *Federal Information Dept.*   Federal and territorial government lists. [1958–62?] Salisbury.   JQ2784.A3

875
_____ Handbook to the Federation of Rhodesia and Nyasaland. [London, Cassell, 1960] 803 p.   DT856.A47

876
The Rhodesia-Zambia-Malawi directory (including Botswana and Moçambique). [1910]+ Bulawayo, Publications (Central Africa). annual.   DT947.R5
   Title varies.

877
Zambia. *Information Services.*   A handbook to the Republic of Zambia. [Lusaka? 1964] 153 p.   DT963.8.A55
   Cover title: *Zambia Today.*

INDEX

Dimock, Marshall E., 3
Directories of Government Agencies (U.S.), 788
Directory of: Albanian Officials, 51; *Bulgarian Government and Party Officials,* 108;
 Bulgarian Officials, 107; *Chinese Communist Officials,* 147; *Czechoslovak Officials,*
 183, 184; *East German Officials,* 271; *Hungarian Officials,* 309; *North Korean Officials,* 416; *Personalities of the Cuban Government,* 169; *Polish Officials,* 594–596,
 604; *Rumanian Officials,* 616; *Soviet Officials,* 757; *U.A.R. Personnages,* 212;
 Ukrainian Officials, 767; *Yugoslav Officials,* 846, 854
Dodd, Clement H., 736
Dombrowski, John, 299
Dominican Republic, 203–206; Oficina Nacional de Administración y Personal, 203
Dominions Office and Colonial Office List, 40
Donaint, Pierre, 529
Donovan, James A., 781.6
Dubai, 772
Duffy, Frank J., 546
Dutch East Indies; *see* Indonesia

East Pakistan; *see* Bangladesh
Eastern Europe, 28
Echeman, Jacques, 250
Eckler, A. Ross, 781.33
Ecuador, 207–210
Egypt, 211–217; Government Press, 213
El Salvador, 218–222
Emmerson, *Sir* Harold, 295.4
Encyclopedia of Governmental Advisory Organizations, 779
Encyclopédie africaine et malgache, 531, 789
Encyclopédie permanente de l'administration française, 251
Encyclopédie politique et constitutionnelle, Série Afrique, 116, 118, 128,
 130, 199, 229, 301, 370, 448, 458, 483, 485, 621, 630, 790
Estes, Thomas S., 781.43
États africains d'expression française et République malgache, 24
Ethiopia, 39, 223–230, 361; Ministry of Information, 225
Europa Encyclopedia, 25
Europa Year Book, 25
Europe, 22, 23, 25
European Governments in Exile, 23, 88, 195, 256, 297, 454, 520, 545, 605, 857
Everhart, William C., 781.31
Executive Register of the United States, 780
Exiled governments (1939–45), 23, 88, 195, 256, 297, 454, 520, 545, 605, 857

Fall, Bernard B., 816, 817
Favoreu, Louis, 485
Ferguson's Ceylon Directory, 663
Fighting French Year Book, 257
Fiji, 231–234
Finland, 235–239; Unesco Toimikunta, 236
Fitch, Edwin M., 781.2, 781.24
France, 240–260; Haut Commissariat de France en Indochine, 812;
 Secrétariat général du gouvernement, 241
France combattante, 258
Free French government, 255–260
French Sudan; *see* Mali
French West Africa, 26, 628
Frome, Michael, 781.30

Tixier, Gilbert, 448
Togo, 33, 34, 716–718; Service du Protocole, 716
Tonga, 719–720
Trans-Jordan, 356, 357, 394, 395
Translation and Secretarial Service, Bangkok, 714
Trapnell, Edward R., 781.42
Trento, Joseph J., 781.36
Trinidad and Tobago, 721–722
Trucial States; *see* United Arab Emirates
Tsien, Tche-Hao, 151
Tudor, Judy, 234
Tung, Lin, 146
Tunisia, 723–729
Turkey, 730–744; Merkezî Hükûmet Teşkilâtı Araştırma Projesi, Yönetim Kurulu, 730–733

Uganda, 745–754; Ministry of Information, Broadcasting and Tourism, 751, 752
Ukraine, 767
Umm al Qaivan, 772
Union of Soviet Socialist Republics, 28, 755–771
United Arab Emirates, 772
United Arab Republic; *see* Egypt
United Committee of South-Slavs in London, 858
United Nations, Public Administration Division, 6
United Nations Directory of National Agencies and Institutions for the improvement of Public Administration, 6
United States, 3, 773–788; AID Mission in Vietnam, Public Administration Division, 830; Agency for International Development, 300; *Agricultural Research Service,* 781.7; *Alaska Railroad,* 781.2; Army, Korea Civil Assistance Command, 429; *Atomic Energy Commission,* 781.42; *Bureau of Labor Statistics,* 781.13; *Bureau of Land Management,* 781.27; *Bureau of Outdoor Recreation,* 781.24; *Bureau of Reclamation,* 781.34; *Bureau of the Budget,* 781.20; *Bureau of the Census,* 781.33; Central Intelligence Agency, 107, 184, 416, 767, 854; Civil Service Commission, 782; *Civil Service Commission,* 781.19; Congress, House, Committee on Government Operations, 784; Congress, Senate, Committee on Government Operations, 775; Consulate General, Hongkong, 152; *Department of Agriculture,* 781.32; *Department of Defense,* 781.11; *Department of Health, Education and Welfare,* 781.39; *Department of Housing and Urban Development,* 781.9; *Department of Justice,* 781.3; *Department of Labor,* 781.37; *Department of State,* 781.43; Dept. of State, Division of Biographic Information, 604, 768; Dept. of the Army, 153, 417; Embassy, Bulgaria, 108; Embassy, Cambodia, 404; Embassy, China, 160; Embassy, Japan, 390; Embassy, Lebanon, 436; Embassy, Malagasy Republic, 461; Embassy, Nepal, 512; Embassy, Sudan, Economic Section, 671; *Environmental Science Services Administration,* 781.8; *Federal Aviation Administration,* 781.5; *Federal Home Loan Bank Board,* 781.17; *Federal Trade Commission,* 781.28; *Foreign Service of the United States,* 781.18; *Forest Service,* 781.30; Government Printing Office, 781.26; *Internal Revenue Service,* 781.25; Library of Congress, 37; *Library of Congress,* 781.38; *National Aeronautics and Space Administration,* 781.36; *National Labor Relations Board,* 781.41; *National Park Service,* 781.31; *National Science Foundation,* 781.16; Office of Strategic Services, Research and Analysis Branch, 113, 254, 591; *Office of Territorial Affairs,* 781.40; Operations Mission to Thailand, Public Administration Division, 714; *Patent Office,* 781.29; *Peace Corps,* 781.22; *Post Office Department,* 781.10; President, 787; *Small Business Administration,* 781.15; *Smithsonian Institution,* 781.21; *Soil Conservation Service,* 781.23; *Tennessee Valley Authority,* 781.35; *United States Air Force,* 781.4; *United States Army,* 781.1; *United States Information Agency,* 781.14; *United States Marine Corps,* 781.6; *United Sates Navy,* 781.12; *United States Postal Service,* 781.10; War Dept., General Staff, 391